You Can Do
CHRISTIAN PUPPETS

A beginner's book of puppet craft
and playscripts

Bea Carlton

Illustrations and puppet craft instructions
by Anne Kircher

MERIWETHER PUBLISHING LTD.
Colorado Springs, Colorado

Meriwether Publishing Ltd., Publisher
P.O. Box 7710
Colorado Springs, CO 80933

Editor: Arthur Zapel
Typesetting: Sharon Garlock
Cover design and illustrations: Anne Kircher

© Copyright MCMLXXXIX Meriwether Publishing Ltd.
Printed in the United States of America
First Edition

Library of Congress Cataloging-in-Publication Data

Carlton, Bea.
    You can do Christian puppets : a beginner's book of puppet craft and play-scripts / by Bea Carlton ; illustrations and puppet craft instructions by Anne Kircher.
        p.   cm.
    ISBN 0-916260-58-5
    1. Puppets and puppet-plays in Christian education. 2. Puppet making.
I. Kircher, Anne.   II. Title.
BV1535.9.P8C37   1989
246'.7 -- dc19   89-3210
                                                                         CIP

DEDICATION

*To my husband — Mark, and friends —
O.V. and Violet Oplinger, for their much
appreciated help with puppet stages and
puppets, and to my daughter, Becky, for her
invaluable help in finishing this book.*

TABLE OF CONTENTS

Foreword

For many years I had an intense desire to use puppets but they hung like tantalizing red apples, wonderfully desirable, but out of my reach. Then a friend invited me to a one-day puppet workshop where I learned how to make and use puppets. I made a puppet, began experimentally to use it and was forever hooked on puppetry!

Those cute little creations quickly became almost real to me. I borrowed Toby, a little blue puppet with bulging eyes, and I became so attached to him it was painful for me to return him to his owner. I sometimes become so involved when I'm doing a puppet play that when a puppet cries I find myself misty eyed and drippy nosed. Many other puppeteers will testify to a similar experience.

I have discovered that people of every age love puppets and relate to them. Pick up a puppet and step behind a screen or puppet stage and even the shy, self-conscious youngster will begin carrying on an earnest and animated conversation with your colorful little puppet helper. Even workers with the elderly are now using puppets to brighten the lonely and empty lives of their patients.

My prayers go with you as you step into the exciting, fun world of puppetry! *You* can do Christian puppets!

Bea Carlton

Introduction

The age we live in is a perilous time for children and youth. The devilish scourges of drugs, alcohol, immorality and rebellion are sweeping the land. Once drawn into these evil whirlpools, many victims never find their way out. It is an important mission for the Christian to rescue as many as possible. Better still, we need to save the innocent from the temptation to follow these evils whose only product is heartbreak and terror.

God has promised if we sow the good seed, his Word, it will accomplish what it was sent to do. Winning children, young people and adults to Christ, and delivering them from the clutches of the adversary is the purpose of the Word of God. So let us get on with the job that is every Christian's responsibility: sowing seed!

One of the most effective tools to use in seed-sowing is puppetry. Almost everyone, young and old alike, loves cute, lovable puppets. That wiggly child, that whispering teenager or that tired adult may "turn off" to a sermon, but give them a lively, bewitching puppet or two in action and you will capture the attention of everyone present.

And *you* can do puppets! No unique talent or training is needed. You need only want to try and you will discover that you can do puppets. The great advantage of using puppets is that they open doors: day-care centers, schools, children's clubs, libraries, hospitals and churches. All welcome a puppet ministry. Puppets are also welcome visitors to the local Sunday school, children's church, vacation Bible school and Bible clubs. A puppet program now and then in the adult service adds an extra spark, puts across a valuable lesson or promotes a special activity. I find that adults often request a puppet play, especially in the morning service. Parks (when permission is granted) are a good place to sow a little gospel seed with puppets. And an entertaining way to advertise your church services.

Children and adults relate to puppets. Puppets are fun to watch. Lessons are absorbed without the child realizing he or she is being taught. Salvation, honesty, love, kindness, and sharing are some lessons easily taught. The dangers and sadness that come from lying, stealing, cheating, alcohol and drug use can be demonstrated as object lessons. Puppets can teach Bible verses, new songs and they show the results of unacceptable behavior.

Since the Bible does not speak of animals going to heaven or accepting Christ as Savior, it is probably best to use only "human" type puppets for praying, accepting the Lord or going to heaven. Animal and other type puppets can, however, be used very effectively to teach character lessons such as honesty, love and kindness.

Puppets are one of the most valuable of all teaching aids but should not be used exclusively. Don't use any one approach all the time or it will become common-place and lose its effectiveness as an attention-grabber. Variety truly is the spice of life. Object lessons, flannelgraph lessons, magic tricks, chalk-talks, films, pantomimes, plays and other aids should all be used along with puppets.

Puppets are entertaining but you must remember to teach a lesson. Don't *just* entertain. Make your puppet script interesting and exciting. It can be funny or serious, or a combination of both, but *do* teach a lesson. Also, a puppet program can be as boring as a dull teacher. Puppets acting out a story are more effective than puppets just telling stories or preaching. If the "telling" is spiced with humor and sound effects, or told in an extremely interesting way, just "talking" is fine but it does require showmanship.

Don't use "goody-goody" characters. They are as hard to "take" on the stage as in real life. Besides, they are not believable. Make your characters fail and then overcome, as real people do. No one likes pious, pompous Christians, and they certainly should not be used as puppet types for your presentations.

SECTION I:
PUPPET CRAFT

CHAPTER ONE

Constructing Papier Mâché Puppets

Puppets are fun to make. And you don't have to be an experienced craftsman to make expressive, delightful puppets! Just reach inside yourself and bring out your youthful enthusiasm and imagination.

The world of puppets includes a broad variety of types. A few of these include stick puppets, shadow puppets, marionettes, finger puppets, sock puppets, paper bag puppets, papier mâché, movable-mouth and even the kind that can be drawn right on the hand. The two types of puppets we will describe in this book are papier mâché puppets and movable-mouth puppets (similar to some of the ones seen on TV's "Sesame Street"). Let's begin!

Preparing An Armature for the Head

To begin with, you need a base or armature for the head upon which to start putting the papier mâché. Use a Styrofoam ball (most craft stores carry many sizes). The Styrofoam ball provides a solid, permanent base and hole for the finger to manipulate the head. A balloon may also be used, but if it is too big you end up with a hollow head which will flop around and be harder to control during play performance. Also, if the papier mâché is not evenly applied on the balloon, you might end up with a weak spot in the head once the balloon is popped. Like humans, no puppet needs a hole in the head.

The best size for the head is around 3" in diameter. Remember to keep the head in relative proportion to the body. Puppets are meant to be caricatures of life and not literal representations. Some leeway in body proportion is okay, but remember, the puppet has to be secure and easy to maneuver during your play performance. The size of the hand operating the puppet will be your key of reference. A head that is too big or a body that is too big may be hard to manipulate.

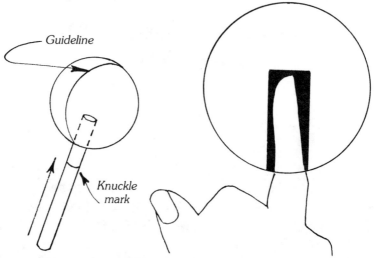

The Styrofoam ball needs to be prepared before papier mâché can be applied. The hole for your forefinger can be made with a dowel rod about ¾" (for an adult finger) in diameter. Mark the equivalent length of your forefinger (down to the second knuckle) on the dowel. This will ensure that you don't push the rod in too far. Slowly work the dowel into the Styrofoam ball up to the mark on the stick, making sure you aim the stick directly towards the center and not off to one side. If the hole needs to be larger, carefully twist the stick to expand the hole slightly outward. In this particular pattern, the neck of the costume will be glued up inside the finger hole, so allow for a little extra room for the material. Your finger should be comfortable yet fairly snug in the hole.

Many of the facial features can be painted on later, but at this time, you may want to attach a simple nose by using a small Styrofoam ball. Mark a spot halfway between the finger hole and the top of the head for the placement of the nose. Place the small ball on this spot on the face and gently twist and push the ball against the large one. The Styrofoam will push in a little creating a dent in which to pour some glue. After the glue and ball are in place, two toothpicks that have been broken off to ¾ length can

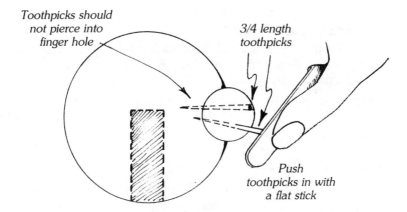

*Toothpicks should
not pierce into
finger hole*

*3/4 length
toothpicks*

*Push
toothpicks in with
a flat stick*

be inserted through the small Styrofoam nose and into the large ball. The toothpicks should be shortened so they do not pierce through into the finger hole. They will hold the nose securely in place. Puppets need to be durable because they may receive a moderate amount of eager abuse at the hands of young children wanting to play with them.

Making and Applying Papier Mâché

The Styrofoam head is soft and easily dented at this point. At least two coats of papier mâché coating are needed to form a protective, durable "skin" for the head. Brown or white packing paper is ideal for use in papier mâché since it is fibrous and tough. You may want to have both kinds, one for each layer so that you know where one layer ends and the other begins. Soak the paper in water to soften it and then work it with your hands to make it pliable.

While the paper is soaking, you can mix the paste. If wheat paste is available (not the same as wheat flour), mix it with water to the consistency of thick cream. It should fall in blobs from a spoon.

Or if you can't get wheat paste, white glue and water also will work when mixed to the consistency of thick cream. Add water slowly to white glue. If the paste becomes too thin you may have to add lots of white glue to thicken it up again.

Squeeze the excess water out of the paper and gently rip the paper into 1½" squares or narrow strips. Paper pieces can be dipped into the glue or rub a dab of glue onto each piece. Paste onto the head, rubbing all edges down. You may need to keep a finger on one corner while rubbing down the others. Additional paste may be needed on the outside. Keep overlapping each piece until the entire head is covered. Rub down any edges that may stick out with a little extra glue. The second layer should be added while the first one is still wet. Follow the same directions as for the first layer. At this time wiggly eyes can be pressed into the wet papier mâché. Be sure to put extra glue on the back of the eye before pressing into the head. Allow the head to dry completely before proceeding to the next step.

Painting the Head

Apply a coat of gesso (available at any art or craft store) to the head before applying the acrylic paint. If the skin is rough, allow the gesso to dry, and then sand it down. Apply a second coat of gesso and let it dry thoroughly.

Acrylic paint is the best paint to use for decorating your puppet because it dries quickly and the colors are rich. Select a skin color and cover the head completely, working paint into all areas. Let it dry completely before going to the next step.

Facial Features and Hair

Now the mouth, eyes (if not already added), and eyebrows can be painted on. The character of the puppet can be conveyed by choosing an appropriate expression for the puppet. See page 20 in the human movable mouth chapter for some ideas on eye expressions. If you have a happy puppet, paint him with a smile, bright eyes, rosy cheeks and raised eyebrows. A sad or mean puppet should probably have a down-turned mouth, furrowed or thick eyebrows, maybe his skin color could even be a little bluish or greenish. Use your imagination.

Once the paint is dry, you can add hair to your puppet. An old, discarded wig can be cut up and used for hair. The wig will be easier to glue if you include the mesh part where the hair is attached into the wig (it may be difficult trying to glue loose hair onto your puppet). Trim the hair to the length you want after it is dry. Long hair can be brushed or combed into different hairdos to create the effect of a different puppet.

Another alternative is yarn or even fake fur for short hair. When using yarn, a full head may take up to 20 to 30 lengths of yarn (lengths may be between 2" to 8"). Apply a wide band of glue where you want the hairline part to be, and then add yarn one strand at a time until the top and back of the head are covered. Once

Glue base of
the skull after the
top has dried

Glue
here

the glue on top has dried, continue to glue down the yarn around the base of the skull so that the hair is attached all the way down to the base of the skull.

Making the Puppet Body

The final step will be making the body. You want the body of the costume to be long enough to cover your forearm so it will not show during the performance. It should also be loose enough to allow for comfortable movement of your arm. The dimensions shown in the illustration should be adjusted to the size of the arm using the puppet. Felt is a good material to use for the body. The edges do not fray, and shapes can be cut out and glued on to suggest buttons or collars without having to hem the edges.

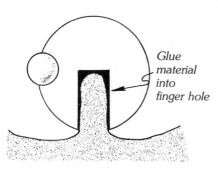

Glue
material
into
finger hole

Cut out the basic pattern and sew a ¼" seam all the way around except for the bottom where the hand slides in. If felt is not used and you have material that will fray, you will want to turn under a hem at the bottom of the skirt. Trim the seam

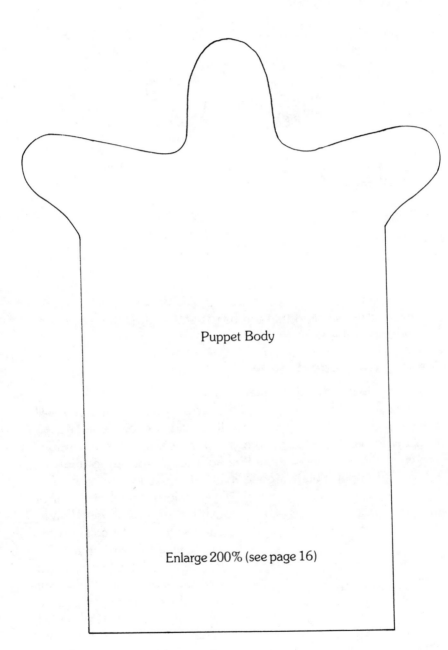

Puppet Body

Enlarge 200% (see page 16)

at the neck which will fit up into the finger hole in the Styrofoam head. When trimming the neck seam, be careful not to cut too close to the seam or it will rip out. You want to eliminate extra bulk in the neck so that your finger will still fit into the finger hole after gluing the fabric body into the finger hole.

Finally, the head and cloth body must be glued together. Pour some glue onto the neck on the cloth body. Wiggle if up into the finger hole in the Styrofoam head. Push the material into place with your finger, making sure the material doesn't come together and close the finger hole when it dries.

Other Alternatives

If you don't have much time to make a puppet, a quicker alternative is to use an old doll head. The body can then be attached to the rubber doll head.

Another approach is to purchase a face from a craft store and a Styrofoam ball which will fit the size of the face. Do not attach a small Styrofoam ball for the nose. Leave the ball plain. Apply the two layers of papier mâché and while it is still wet, press the face into the papier mâché. You may want to add some extra glue to the back of the face before you press it on to ensure it is firmly attached. Hair will need to be attached after the papier mâché dries.

CHAPTER TWO
Constructing Movable-Mouth Puppets

    The puppets described in this section are the kind that were made popular by the television show, "Sesame Street." If you want a puppet that is more lifelike and able to move its mouth and "talk," then these instructions are for you. A little knowledge of sewing helps, but it is not absolutely necessary. These puppets are simple enough that they can be hand sewn if a sewing machine is not readily available. Please read these instructions all the way through before purchasing materials and constructing the puppets.

Fabric Selection and Color Usage
    Select a material that is durable and non-fraying if possible. Felt works well for this purpose. It usually comes in bolts about 72" wide. If your fabric store carries this width, you will need about ½ yard of material for one human/frog puppet. If the material is in a narrower width, purchase a yard of material for each puppet. The mouth should always be in a contrasting, yet harmonious color to the body. Most fabric and craft stores sell 12" squares of felt in a wide variety of colors. These can be purchased to create the mouth, tongue and any other facial features. Or use the felt for finishing touches you wish to add to the costuming.
    Choose material that has a pattern or color appropriate to the character of your puppet. You may want to select fake fur for an animal puppet or a plain, colored fabric for a human puppet. The colors do not have to be realistic in nature. Remember puppets are caricatures of life and not literal representations. Color can be used

to represent the personality of a puppet. Yellow may indicate happiness, blue may show sadness or melancholy, red for anger, green for jealousy, etc.

The human puppet can be dressed with different outfits over the main body. If you are going to dress the human puppet in different costumes, you may want to make the body a neutral color to coordinate with different outfits. Changing costumes allows the puppeteer to convert one puppet into several different characters to adapt to different plays. Different hairpieces or hats can be pinned onto the head to add to the effect of the costume. Purchase doll clothes, secondhand baby or toddler clothing, or sew your own costumes. Design your puppets around your play-use needs.

Enlarging Pattern Pieces

All pattern pieces for the movable-mouth puppets will need to be enlarged 200% in order to make full-sized puppets for an adult hand. They cannot be used the same size they are printed in this book. Most quick print and copier shops have copier machines that will enlarge to 200% for about 15 cents a copy. This is the easiest and quickest way to enlarge the pattern pieces to the correct size. After they have been enlarged, pin them to the material and cut the pieces out that you need.

Making the Human and Frog Puppets

Pattern pieces for these puppets are found on pages 23-25.

Have the pages enlarged 200% at a copier shop as described on the preceding page. Read each pattern piece carefully to see if the piece needs to be placed on a fold or how many times a piece needs to be cut out. Some only need one piece. Others may need to be cut out as many as four times. Fabric can be doubled over in order to cut two at a time. Also, throughout these instructions, you will be stitching ¼" seams unless directed to do otherwise.

Begin with the "head" (piece #1). You should have cut out two of these. Mark the darts onto the wrong side of each piece with chalk or a light pencil line. Sew the darts on both pieces. Next, take the "nose" (either 2A or 2B, depending on how big you want to make it). If you are making a frog, omit this part explaining the nose. You should have two pieces for the nose. Stitch right sides together, leaving the notched end open. Turn the nose right side

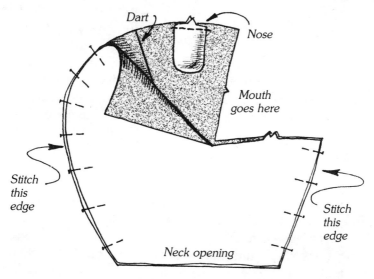

Dart

Nose

Mouth goes here

Stitch this edge

Stitch this edge

Neck opening

out and stuff with poly-fill. Pin the nose, matching notches, above the mouth as shown in the illustration. Now take the second piece of #1 and with the right sides together, pin the two together, leaving the mouth and neck open. Stitch both seams. When sewing, go slowly over the nose. This part has four layers of material and may be more difficult to sew.

Next, prepare the "mouth"

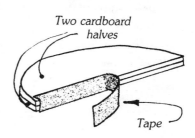

Two cardboard halves

Tape

(piece #3). You will need to cut a cardboard mouth in addition to a fabric mouthpiece. Take a piece of 2- or 3-ply cardboard or white poster board. (Do not use colored poster board. The color may bleed through the material when it is glued. Do not use corrugated cardboard because it is too bulky.) This cardboard will function as the inside lining of the mouth. After the cardboard circle is cut out, cut it in half along the diameter following the dashed lines. Use duct tape to retape the pieces together to form a secure joint. Double the pieces over and tape the two together at the center cut (see illustration). This will ensure that the mouth will lie flat when it is folded over. It will not work well enough to just fold the cardboard over. The joint has to move loosely and also lie flat.

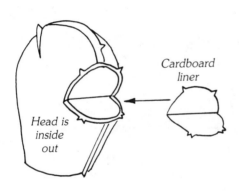

Cardboard
liner

Head is
inside
out

Pin the fabric mouth into the head, matching notches. Stitch a seam all the way around the mouth. Leaving the head piece inside out, glue the cardboard onto the mouthpiece. Use a clear liquid glue. Use moderation with the glue. If you apply too much, the glue may soak through the material and show on the other side. Press the material down to eliminate any wrinkles in the cloth. Clamp clothespins around the mouth while it is drying to hold it in place. Allow the cardboard to dry before turning the head right side out; otherwise, the cardboard may pull away from the fabric when you try to turn it right side out. You may have to slightly bend the cardboard a little bit to get it to turn right side out. It can be straightened out once it is right side out.

The cardboard piece should stick out about ¼" past the mouthpiece, creating the effect of lips when it is turned right side out. Glue the tongue in place. The mouth is now finished.

Next, take the "puppet

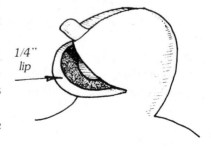

1/4"
lip

body" (piece #5). Pin the right sides of the material together at the shoulder seams. Stitch a ¼" seam. Pin the side seams and stitch together, leaving the armholes open. Hem the bottom edge of the puppet body skirt with a ½" hem.

Now select the "hand" pattern piece appropriate to your puppet (pieces 7A-non-human, 7B-frog hand, 7C-human hand). Cut the fingers out first as a solid block that looks like a mitten. Now take the puppet arm (piece #6). You should have four of these cut out. For each complete arm, you will need two sides. If you are using a material such as felt, where there is not an obvi-ous right or wrong side, you will need to be sure that each side is the reverse of the other be-fore sewing them together. Otherwise, you may end up with a wrong side and a right side that can't be matched so that both right sides face out.

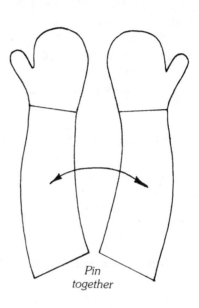

Pin together

The fingers can be cut apart after they have been stitched.

Pin the hand to the wrist of the puppet arm matching notches and keeping the right sides together. Stitch the arm and hand together. Repeat this on all four pieces.

With right sides of both arms pinned togeth-er, take the hand pattern piece and place it on the material. Using chalk or a light pencil line, trace the fingers onto the hand. This will be your guide for stitch-ing the fingers. Use a smaller seam than ¼" on the fingers. Stitch the arm and

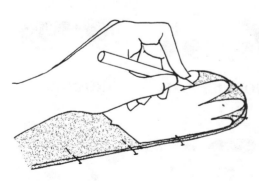

the hand together all in one seam. You may want to sew the fingers twice to give them extra durability. Cut the fingers apart after stitching. Be careful not to cut too close to the seam when cutting the fingers.

Turn the whole arm right side out. This piece will be narrow and it may take a little work to get everything turned right side out. Use a safety pin or some other instrument to help you pull things out. Once it is right side out, push the poly-fill stuffing down into the arm with a long narrow dowel rod. Fill up the arm with poly-fill.

A short seam can be sewn across the elbow to keep the stuffing inside the arm and to create a joint for the arm to bend at.

Once both arms are finished, pin them into the armholes on the puppet body. The thumbs should point in towards the body. Stitch seams together. If this armhole is too small to sew on your machine, stitch it by hand.

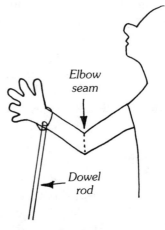

After the puppet is finished, a small dowel rod or clothes hanger cut to the desired length can be secured to the puppet's wrist with a rubber band or wire. The puppeteer can then move the stick to move the puppet's arm. Obviously, you can only do one arm if there is only one puppeteer.

Pin the neck of the body onto the neck of the puppet head. Stitch together with a ¼" seam.

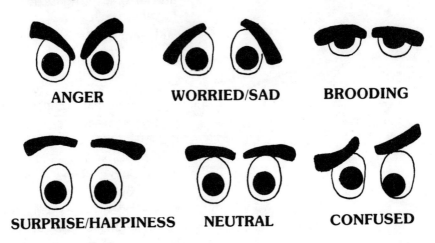

ANGER   **WORRIED/SAD**   **BROODING**

SURPRISE/HAPPINESS   **NEUTRAL**   **CONFUSED**

Turn the whole puppet right side out.

The finishing touches will be to add the facial features. Wiggly eyes or frog eyes can be purchased at a craft store. Or, using scraps of felt, you can cut out eyes and eyebrows from felt. Play around with the placement of the eyebrows. It does a lot to suggest the expression of a puppet.

For the hair, depending on the character of the puppet, you may want to use yarn, part of a wig or fake fur.

Secondhand wigs can be purchased at thrift stores, garage or rummage sales. Or sometimes a well-stocked craft store will sell packages of material that looks like curly hair and can be used on the head or as a beard.

Lastly, you will need to make two more parts, a small pillow to insert into the head and foam rubber liner for the body, so that the puppet will hold its shape.

To make the pillow, begin by cutting out two #8 pieces and one #9 which is placed on a fold. Sew the darts on each piece first. After the darts are sewn, pin right sides together and stitch a ¼" seam along the top edge.

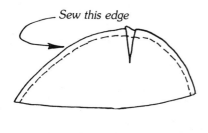

Sew this edge

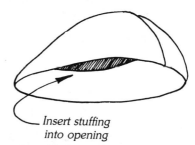

Insert stuffing
into opening

Pin piece #9 to the bottom edge of the piece you just sewed together. This will form the complete pillow. When stitching the

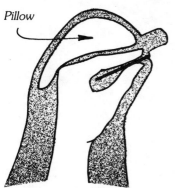

Pillow

seam of the piece that forms the bottom, leave about 3" on one side unstitched. This will provide an opening into the pillow in which to insert the poly-fill stuffing. After you have stuffed the pillow, close the opening by hand with a whip stitch. This pillow then fits up into the head of the puppet to help it keep its shape.

For the foam rubber stuffing, cut a piece of 1" foam rubber in one piece 7" x 16½" long. Cut the edge of the foam rubber at a 45° angle. Glue that edge together, clamping it in place with clothespins while it is drying.

When it is dry, insert it into the body. It should fit snugly and hold in place even when your arm is not in the puppet.

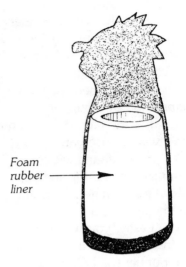

Foam rubber liner

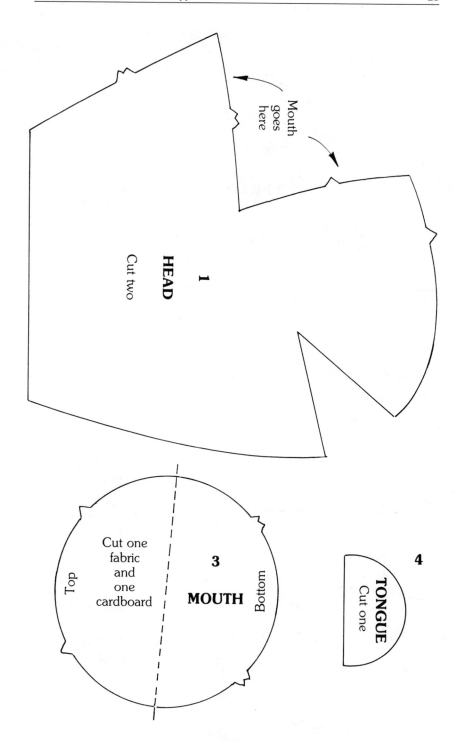

Mouth
goes
here

Cut two

HEAD

1

Cut one
fabric
and
one
cardboard

Top

3

MOUTH

Bottom

4

TONGUE
Cut one

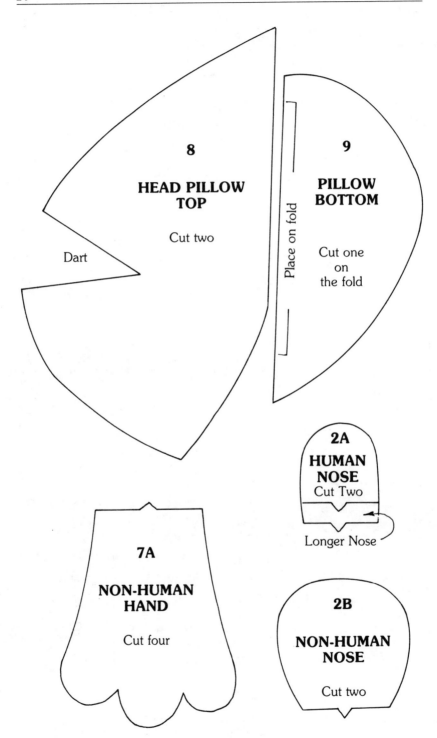

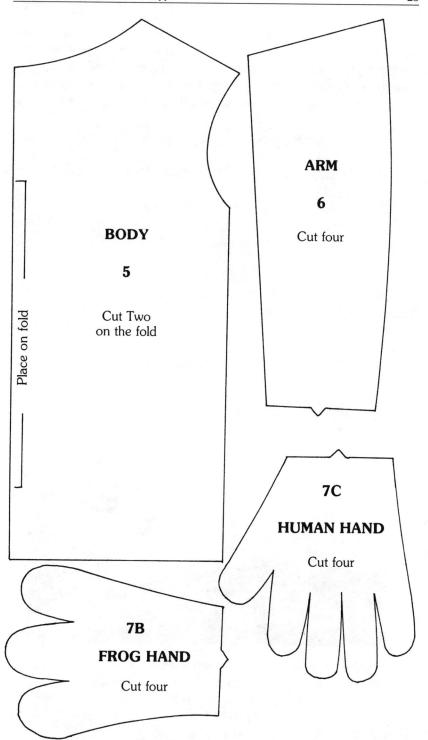

BODY

5

Cut Two
on the fold

Place on fold

ARM

6

Cut four

7C

HUMAN HAND

Cut four

7B

FROG HAND

Cut four

The instructions included in this section are for the snake and turtle puppets with movable mouths. The snake is probably the simplest puppet to make of this movable-mouth kind. It's a good one to begin with if this is your first attempt at sewing a puppet.

The pattern pieces you will need for the snake and the turtle are:

<table>
<tr><td>Snake Puppet Pieces</td><td>Turtle Puppet Pieces</td></tr>
<tr><td>A, B, C, G, H, I, J</td><td>A, B, C, D, E, F, I, J, K, L</td></tr>
</table>

Enlarge the pattern pieces found on pages 31-33 at 200%. Directions for enlarging the patterns are found on page 16. Also, all seams mentioned should be sewn ¼" wide unless directed to do otherwise.

See the beginning section on movable-mouth puppets which covers the selection of appropriate fabric and colors. The snake puppet does not require much material and large scraps of felt can be used if you have them on hand. Or, if you need to purchase material, ½ yard should be more than enough. You will probably have fabric left over for other puppets.

The Snake Puppet

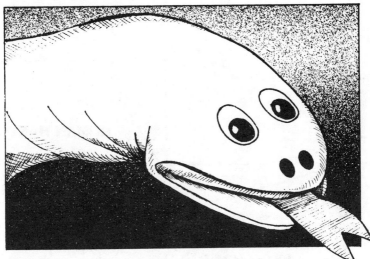

Once you have the enlarged pattern pieces, pin them onto the material and cut the pattern pieces out. Before cutting, read each piece carefully to see if it needs to be placed on a fold or if it needs to be cut out more than once. The fabric can be doubled over to cut two pieces out at a time.

Begin with piece A (the head) and piece C (the body). Matching notches, pin the right sides together. Stitch the seam together.

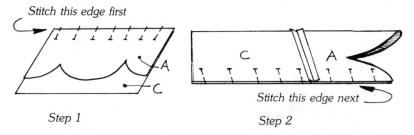

Stitch this edge first

Step 1

Stitch this edge next

Step 2

Next, keeping the right sides together, fold the same piece over length-wise, keeping right sides together. Stitch along the bottom edge. Leave this piece inside out.

Take piece B (the mouth). With right sides together, pin the mouth into the main body. Stitch all the way around the mouth.

You will need to make a cardboard liner for the mouth. Obtain either two- or three-ply cardboard or plain white poster board. *Do not* use corrugated cardboard (it is too bulky) or colored poster board. The color may bleed through the material when gluing. Cut the cardboard mouth in half along the dashed line indicated on the pattern.

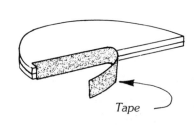

Tape

Place the two cardboard pieces on top of each other as they would lie when the mouth is closed. Tape the two pieces back together along the center fold line. (Be sure to use duct tape or strapping tape, and *not* a paper or Scotch tape.) This will ensure that the mouth will move easily, lie flat, and provide a durable joint for the mouth.

Using a clear liquid glue, cover one side of the cardboard mouth with glue. Put the glue on the side that has no tape. If you put too much glue on, it may soak through the material, so use moderation.

Now insert the cardboard into the fabric mouth that has been sewn into the head. Press the fabric down into the cardboard to make sure it is lying flat and will dry onto the cardboard. The cardboard piece can be clipped in place with clothespins while it is drying. Be sure to let it dry thoroughly. If you try to turn it right side out before the cardboard is finished drying, the cardboard may pull

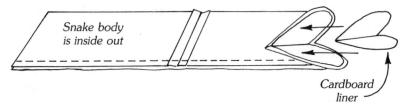

apart from the fabric.

While the puppet is still inside out, turn under a ½" hem at the bottom skirt of the body and sew with a hemming stitch. Or if you are in a hurry, just sew a regular seam on the machine about ⅜" in from the bottom.

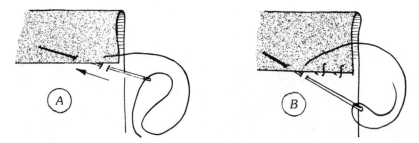

Once the glue has dried, turn the whole puppet right side out.

The finishing touches for the snake will be to add the eyes, tongue and nostrils. These can all be cut out of scraps of felt and glued in place.

The Turtle Puppet

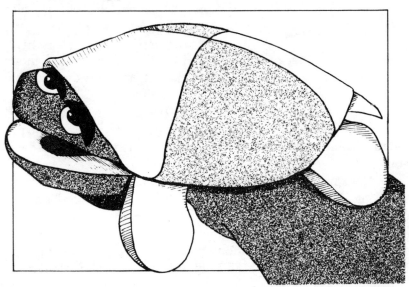

To create the turtle puppet, you will need to follow the same steps that you would for the snake. The snake body is the base for the turtle. You will be adding a "shell" with legs onto the snake body to create the turtle. You will also be putting different facial features on the turtle.

So at this point you should make the basic snake body, following the instructions listed on pages 26-28.

Take pattern piece D (the legs). You will be making four legs, so you should have eight pieces cut out. The underside of the legs can be cut out in a contrasting color. Pin the right sides of each leg together and stitch the seam, leaving the notched end open. After each leg is sewn together, fill each leg with a tablespoon or two of dried beans to weight them a little. This will help them to hang down when in use.

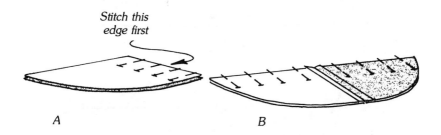

Stitch this edge first

A   B

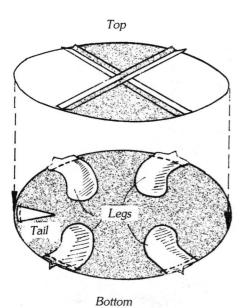

Top

Legs

Tail

Bottom

Next, take the pattern piece (E). You should have four cut out for the top, two in one color and two in another. Pin each quarter part to another quarter part, and then stitch together. Once you have two halves, pin the halves together and stitch a seam to connect the two halves. This should form a circle for the top part of the shell.

Piece "L" will form the bottom of the shell. Pin the legs onto the right side of piece "L", matching notches. At this time you will also need to pin the tail onto this bottom half. See illustration for placement of pieces.

Take the top part of the shell and pin it to the bottom piece with the legs and tail on the inside. Stitch the top half and the bottom half together, leaving about 3" unstitched. You need to leave an opening so that you can turn the shell inside out.

Once you have turned the shell right side out, stuff with enough poly-fill to give it some shape. Close the hole by hand with a whip stitch.

The shell will be attached to the body with a few whip stitches around the shell. Do this part by hand and not on the machine.

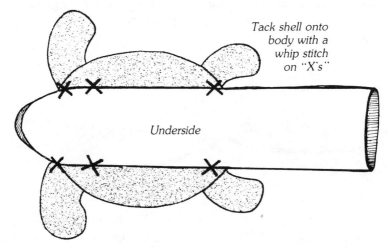

Tack shell onto body with a whip stitch on "X's"

Underside

The final step will be to glue the eyes on and the tongue into the mouth. See page 20 in the human puppet section for ideas on how to make expressive eyes.

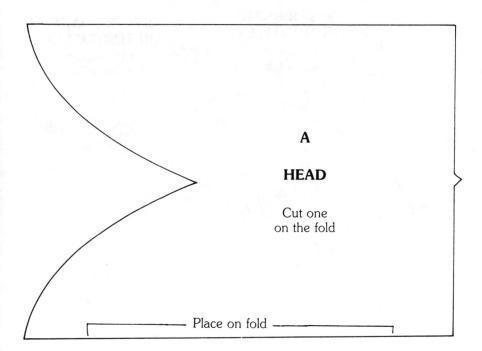

A

HEAD

Cut one
on the fold

—— Place on fold ——

C

BODY

Cut one
on the fold

—— Place on fold ——

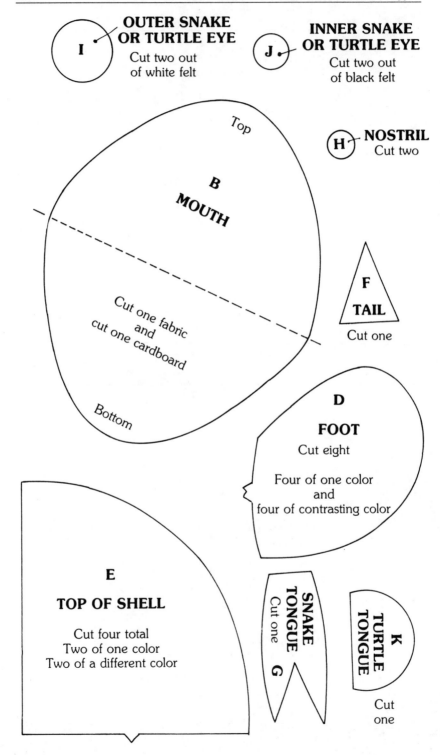

OUTER SNAKE OR TURTLE EYE
Cut two out of white felt

I

INNER SNAKE OR TURTLE EYE
Cut two out of black felt

J

NOSTRIL
Cut two

H

Top

B MOUTH

Cut one fabric and cut one cardboard

Bottom

F TAIL
Cut one

D FOOT
Cut eight

Four of one color and four of contrasting color

E TOP OF SHELL

Cut four total
Two of one color
Two of a different color

SNAKE TONGUE
Cut one
G

K TURTLE TONGUE
Cut one

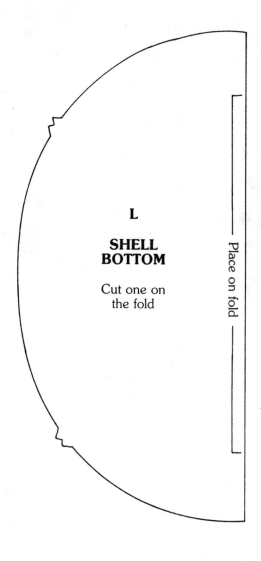

L

**SHELL
BOTTOM**

Cut one on
the fold

Place on fold

**TURTLE
EYEBROW**
(Optional)

Making an Animal Puppet

DOG

FOX

MOUSE

The instructions in this section cover animal puppets with movable mouths. Please read these instructions through before purchasing materials and beginning construction. Also, all seams mentioned should be sewn ¼" wide unless indicated otherwise.

Cut out all of the pieces you will need for the animal puppet, selecting either the dog, fox or mouse pattern pieces. There will be different ears, tongues, eyes and noses for each different animal. The pieces needed for each different animal are as follows:

Dog Puppet Pieces	Fox Puppet Pieces
A, C, E, F, I, J, M, O	A, B, E, G, H, K, L, M, O

Mouse Puppet Pieces

A, D, E, G, J, M, O

Each piece clearly indicates which animal it is for. Also, some pieces may need to be cut out several times or placed on a fold. Read each piece carefully for specific cutting instructions for that piece.

Begin with the ear piece [either B (fox), C (dog), or D (mouse)]. The ears require contrasting material for the inside of the ear. Small 12" squares of felt may be purchased at craft or fabric stores for this purpose. They come in a variety of colors.

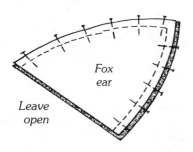

Fox
ear

Leave
open

Pin the right sides together. Sew a seam around the top edges. Leave the bottom seam open for turning right sides out. This is an optional step, but the ears can be stuffed with a little bit of poly-fill after turning right side out. This helps the ear to keep its shape. Do not fill the ears too full or they will not look like animal ears.

Next, take piece "A" (the head). You should have two "A" pieces. Mark the dart on the wrong side of the material with chalk or a light pencil line. Slit the material along the inside dart line. Pin the ear into this dart on the right side of the material. Look at the pattern piece to see how to place the ear. Be sure to lay the inside of

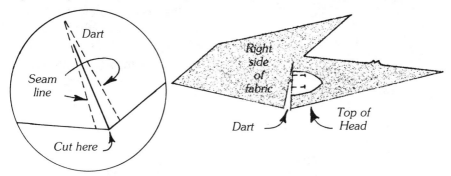

the ear (the contrasting material side) face down. This will ensure that the ears will be facing the correct direction when turned inside out. For the fox and dog puppet, you can fold down a small corner of the ear closest to the top of the head (see illustration). Stitch the dart, tapering your seam as you reach the inside edge (see pattern for seam line). There will be four layers of material where the ear will be stitched, so go slowly over this area with your sewing machine.

Sew an ear onto each side of the head. Next, with right sides together, pin the two "A" pieces together. (If the ear sticks out past the edge of the material where you need to sew, temporarily pin it back out of the way while you are sewing this seam.) Stitch together the top and back of the head (the two sides with the double notch) and the seam that makes the bottom of the chin. Leave the mouth and neck open. Refer to the illustration if you are confused about

which seams to sew to-
gether.

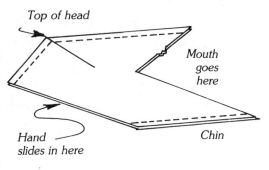

Top of head

Mouth
goes
here

Hand
slides in here

Chin

Next, pin the mouth-
piece (E) into the head,
matching notches. Stitch
seams together.

The mouth will need
an inside cardboard lining.
Use either two- or three-
ply cardboard or white
poster board. Do not use
colored poster board. The color may bleed through your material
when it is glued.

Cut the cardboard mouth apart on the line indicated on the
pattern. With the two pieces
folded over like they would be
when the mouth is closed, tape
the pieces together with duct tape
or electrical tape. This will ensure
that the mouthpiece will move
freely and also lie flat when
closed.

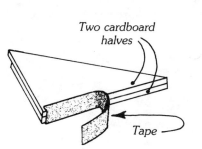

Two cardboard
halves

Tape

Cover the cardboard with
clear glue. (If you use too much,

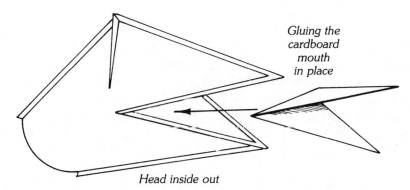

Gluing the
cardboard
mouth
in place

Head inside out

it may soak through the material and show on the outside. Use
moderation.) Insert it into the mouth. Press the fabric down making
sure there are no wrinkles and that it is positioned correctly. Trim
the cardboard down if it sticks out past the seam line of the mouth.
Clothespins can be used to clip the cardboard in place while it is
drying. Let the glue dry for a while. If you try to turn it right side out too

soon, the cardboard may pull away from the fabric.

Turn the whole head right side out once the glue is dry. The cardboard may need to be bent a little to turn the head right side out. It can be flattened out again once it is right side out. Glue the tongue in place in the bottom half of the mouth.

Next, take piece "M" (the body). Stitch the side seam together. Leave this body piece inside out.

Take the head and work it up into the neck from the inside. Pin the head into place. Right sides should be together. Stitch the neck seam together.

Turn up a ½" hem around the bottom of the body and sew in a hem. Use either a hemming stitch or regular stitch.

Turn the whole puppet right side out.

You will now need to glue eyes onto the head. You can purchase wiggly eyes at a craft store, or cut eyes out of scraps of felt. See pattern pieces for the fox eyes. Or, if you purchase wiggly eyes, you can glue a black felt piece to the back of the eye before gluing onto the head. You can glue eyelashes onto the felt if you like.

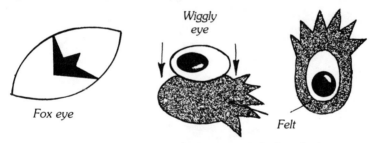

Wiggly eye

Fox eye

Felt

Next, add the nose. If you want to include whiskers, sew or glue them on.

The final step is to make the foam rubber liners for the head and body. This helps the puppet hold its shape so the material does not sag and look baggy.

Take pattern piece "O" and trace it onto a piece of 1" thick foam rubber. Cut out and push up into the top of the head as shown in the illustration on page 38.

Next, cut a piece for the body using the 1" thick foam rubber. Cut the edges at a 45° angle. Glue the edges together and clamp in place with a clothespin while it is drying. This piece will fit into the lower body as shown in the illustration.

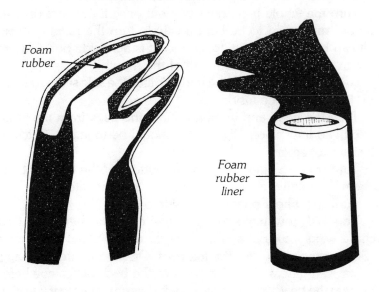

Foam
rubber

Foam
rubber
liner

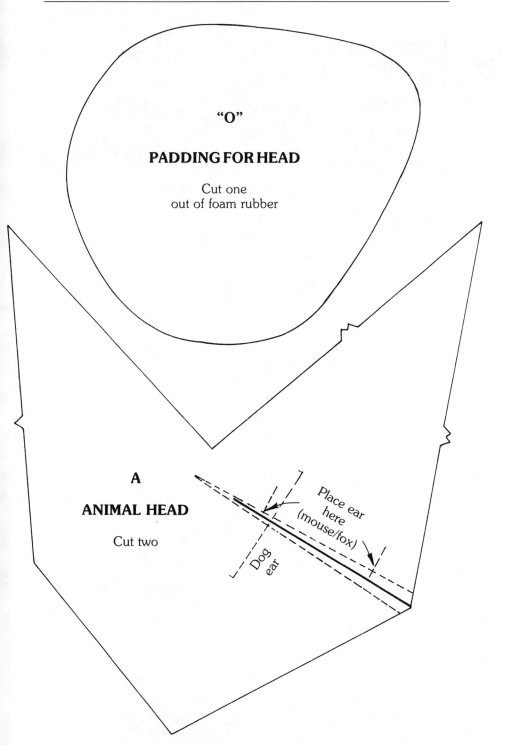

"O"

PADDING FOR HEAD

Cut one
out of foam rubber

A

ANIMAL HEAD

Cut two

Place ear
here
(mouse/fox)

Dog
ear

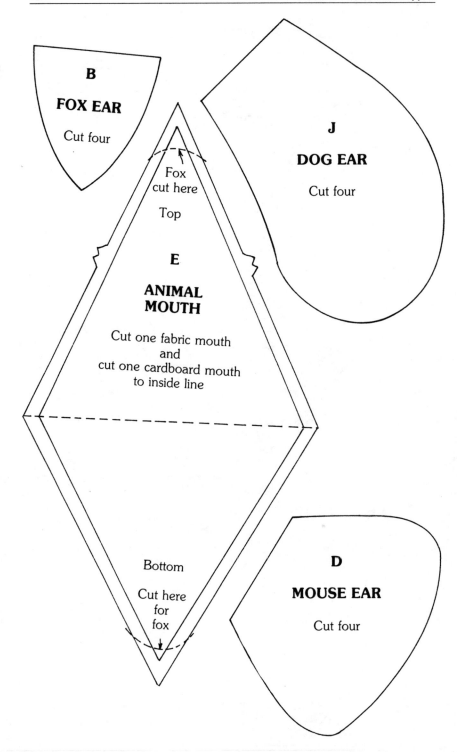

B

FOX EAR

Cut four

Fox
cut here

Top

E

**ANIMAL
MOUTH**

Cut one fabric mouth
and
cut one cardboard mouth
to inside line

J

DOG EAR

Cut four

Bottom

Cut here
for
fox

D

MOUSE EAR

Cut four

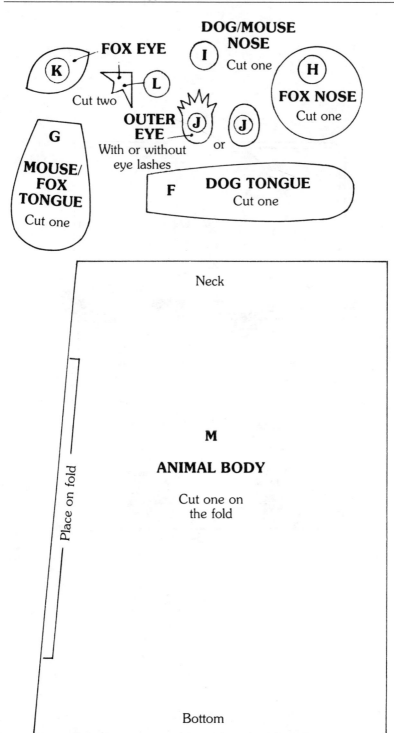

FOX EYE

K

Cut two

DOG/MOUSE NOSE

I

Cut one

H

FOX NOSE

Cut one

L

OUTER EYE

With or without eye lashes

J   or   J

G

MOUSE/ FOX TONGUE

Cut one

F   DOG TONGUE

Cut one

Neck

Place on fold

M

ANIMAL BODY

Cut one on the fold

Bottom

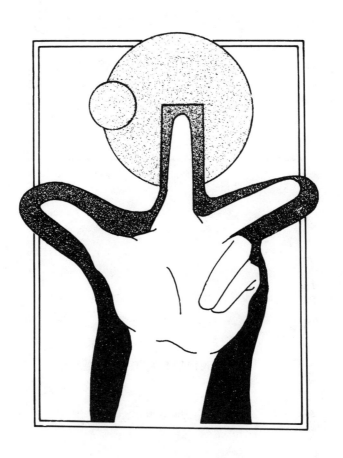

CHAPTER THREE
Using Your Puppets

Puppet Voices & Movements

For all styles of puppets, you will need to develop several different voices in addition to your regular speaking voice: a nasal tone, a high falsetto voice, a deep voice, and different foreign accents, if necessary, for your play. Practice changing back and forth between voice ranges.

Operating the Movable-Mouth Puppet

If you will be using the movable-mouth puppets, the next step you will need to do is to coordinate the voice with the movement of

the mouth. An easy way to begin is to have your puppet mouth along with a song on the radio for practice. Add body movements to the rhythm of the music once you are comfortable with the mouth movements.

Practice opening and closing the mouth much like you would when speaking. (See illustration for how the hand should fit into the puppet head.) However, you don't need to open and close the mouth on every syllable. You don't want a snapping effect. Move the puppet around, adding a tilt to the head. If the children are sitting on the floor below the level of the stage, tilt the puppet's heads downward so the kids can see the whole puppet face.

If you are using a movable-mouth puppet with a rod attached to an arm, practice moving the mouth and arm to achieve the gestures you want. If you have to use both hands to operate your puppet, you may want to lay each page of your script out on the shelf below the stage opening so you don't have to turn pages. (That is if you are using the stage described in the puppet stage construction section.)

Operating the Papier Mâché Puppet

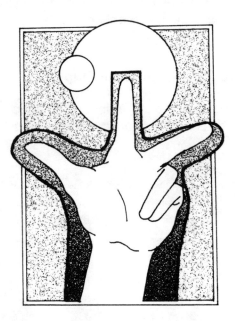

The hand operates differently in the papier mâché puppet than it would in the movable-mouth puppet. You will use the three-fingered position as shown in the illustration. The index finger slides up into the finger hole, and the middle finger and thumb fit into the puppet arms. The remaining two fingers are curled over into the palm.

With the use of your fingers in the puppet arms, you are free to pick up objects and create gestures with the puppet.

Scripts and Programs

Some puppeteers prefer to ad-lib their own skits. But if you are not one of these types of puppeteers, you may prefer to use a script. With the words in front of you, you can concentrate more on the puppet movements and their speaking voices.

You may want to plan programs around special occasions like Mother's Day, Valentine's Day, Thanksgiving, Easter, Christmas. Or, puppet plays help in teaching lessons for Sunday school or vacation Bible school. Several scripts for these uses are included in Section II of this book. Others are available from Contemporary Drama Service, Box 7710, Colorado Springs, CO 80933, (719) 594-4422.

Props

Here are a few examples of props used in the scripts following in Section II. Of course, you will have to find items available in your own area, but these will give you an idea of where to begin.

A little white stuffed dog plays the part of the injured dog in "A Modern Good Samaritan."

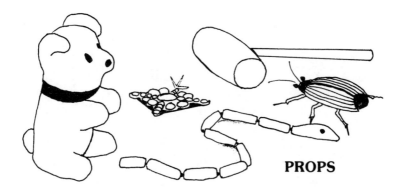

PROPS

The large brooch is Grandma's pin in "Where's That Pin?"

The wooden mallet is used in "A Foolish Young Man." It can be secured to Noah's hand and arm with rubber bands for the ark building scene.

The jointed plastic snake and large black plastic beetle are used in "Happy Jack Attends Church." The snake can be attached to a wire rod and manipulated in such a way that it moves like a real snake.

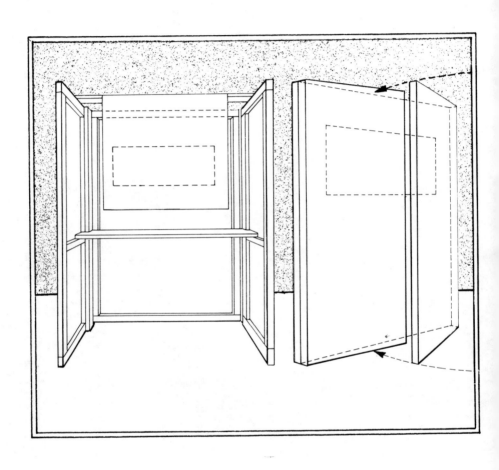

CHAPTER FOUR

Building a Folding Puppet Stage

Materials Needed

Ten 8-foot 1" x 2" boards for frame
Aluminum flashing or corner braces
1½" nails with large heads
Drill and ⅛" bit
Nails and hammer
Staple gun and heavy duty staples
½" plywood
Thin fabric or window tint
Large pieces of corrugated cardboard, fabric or wood paneling

Begin by measuring and cutting 1" x 2" boards to the measurements specified in the drawing on page 50. Measurements for the shelf are based on the 1" x 2" boards being nailed together on the 1" side. Add glue to the corners before nailing them together. To secure each joint and to keep it square, screw in corner braces

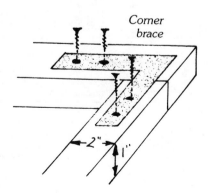

Corner brace

2"

1"

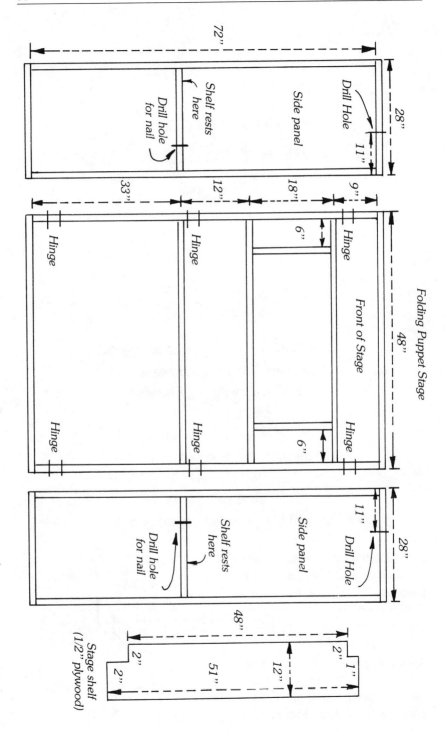

Folding Puppet Stage

72"

28"

Side panel

Drill Hole

11"

Drill hole
for nail

Shelf rests
here

33"   12"   18"   9"

Hinge   Hinge   Front of Stage   Hinge

48"

6"

6"

Hinge   Hinge   Hinge

11"

Drill Hole

28"

Side panel

Shelf rests
here

Drill hole
for nail

Stage shelf
(1/2" plywood)

48"

2"

1"

12"

51"

2"

2"

after they have been nailed. Or if corner braces are not available, cut 2" x 3" strips from aluminum flashing. Staple the strips several times on each side of the joint to secure it firmly in place. Use heavy duty staples in your staple gun.

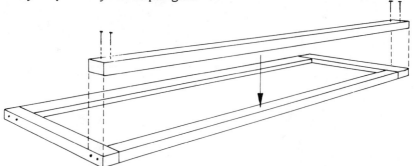

On the left side panel (as the puppeteer would view from the back), place a second 1" x 2" board on top of the first 1" x 2" in the frame. This is needed so that when the two side panels are folded, the left panel will fit over the right panel.

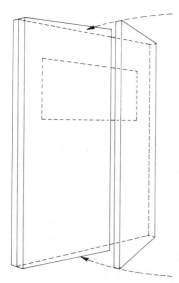

Now the three frames are ready to hinge together. Evenly space three hinges down each side of the inside of the theatre. The panels should fold in towards the back during storage.

After the frames have been hinged together, the three panels are ready to be covered on the outside. Thin wood paneling can be used if your budget allows it. Keep in mind that you will need to cut out a hole on the front panel for the stage opening. Wood paneling may present a few problems under certain circumstances. Sometimes wood paneling may warp. Also, if you need to move your stage from location to location for different performances, wood paneling may make the stage too heavy to haul around comfortably. Another alternative is covering the frame with large pieces of corrugated cardboard or with lightweight but opaque fabric. Fabric can be stretched around the back of the frame and stapled, much like an artist's canvas. If you use cardboard, you can cover it with wallpaper or contact paper.

Next, the stage shelf should have notches cut in the two front corners. Remember that the left side notch should be cut 2" x 2" to allow for the double boards on the left frame. The right side notch should be 1" x 2" (see pattern).

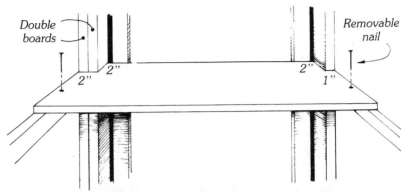

Now set the stage upright with the side panels positioned at right angles to the front panel. Place the stage shelf on the center boards that are 33" from the floor of the stage. Measure 11" from the front on both sides. This is where you will drill a ⅛" hole. Clamp board in place or have someone hold it steady while you drill a hole through both the shelf and the frame board. This will ensure that the holes are evenly aligned. Once the stage is put up for use, long nails or pins will slip into the holes and keep the shelf in place. This shelf will be used by the puppeteer to place the script and puppets on during the play performance.

The curtain backdrop is the last step in building your stage. Use a 1" x 2" board cut 51" long for the curtain rod.

The screen requires material that is thin enough or has an open weave such that the puppeteer can see the puppets through the material, but will not let the audience see you. Also, you do not want your voice to be muffled by the screen. A simple test will let you know if the material will work. In a well-lit room, hold up a piece of the cloth close to your eyes. Now move and wiggle your hands about two feet in front of you like you would a puppet. If you can see clearly, the next step is to check to see if the audience can see you. Have two people look on the other side to verify this.

Cut the material (the edges of the cloth will need to be hemmed) or sun screen approximately 44" x 32". Staple curtain onto rod. Lay the curtain rod across the top of the side panels, about 11" back from the front panel. Hold board securely in place and drill a ⅛" hole through the curtain rod and the frame. Drop a nail or right angle pin through the hole in both boards. The rod will be held in place, while also allowing for interchangeable scenery backdrops for each different play.

Lastly, a light can be clipped on top of each side of the stage-front so that it shines down on the puppets and screen. Adjust so that the puppets and scripts below on the shelf are illuminated, but the puppeteer is still hidden.

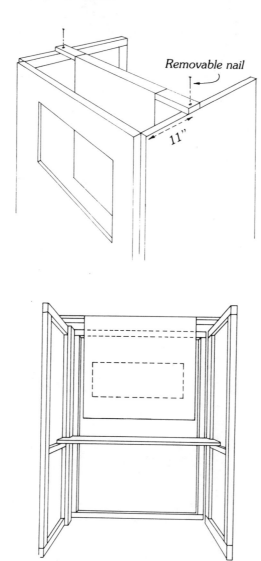

Removable nail

11"

SECTION II:
PLAYSCRIPTS

Scripts and Programs

Many puppeteers ad-lib most of their programs, but most of the time I prefer a script. With the words in front of me, I don't have to concentrate so much on what the puppets are saying and can give more attention to how I'm moving them.

There are many puppet plays on the market and you may choose to use these exclusively. But writing your own scripts, or having someone else write them, usually works well, too. Real life situations, Bible storybooks, puppet books, kids' records or cassettes are good sources for ideas. Scripts for special days: Mother's Day, Valentine's Day, Thanksgiving, Easter, Christmas, are excellent opportunities for puppet plays. Many scripts of this type are available from Contemporary Drama Service, Box 7710, Colorado Springs, CO 80933.

Following are several types of puppet plays for your use. No permission for performance is needed except the purchase of this book. You may reproduce copies for other performers in your group or your church if you like, but performance rights are not transferable to others outside your group or church to whom you may loan your copy of this book. Performance rights will be granted to them with the purchase of this book.

The categories of puppet plays included here are: Old Testament Puppet Plays, Church Life Plays, Christian Behavior Plays, New Testament Bible Lessons, Special Day Scripts and object lessons featuring The Special Problems of Puppet People.

CHAPTER 5

Old Testament Puppet Plays

- The Deceiver
- A Foolish Young Man
- Man Overboard

The Deceiver

Three Puppets: ADAM, EVE, SERPENT

> *(A small tree with little, bright fruit should be on puppet stage. A small tree branch, placed so it can be seen by audience is fine, with artificial fruit, or fruit made from papier mâché and colored brightly. Two pieces should be attached loosely so EVE and ADAM may remove them easily.)*
>
> *(ADAM and EVE should be hand puppets — the glove-type where the fingers of the puppeteer work the little arms of the puppets so they can remove and handle fruit. A large toy serpent — from which part of the head and neck stuffing has been removed so a hand can be inserted — may be used for SERPENT puppet.)*
>
> *(A garden scene may be painted onto a curtain and used as a background, if desired.)*

ANNOUNCER: **The story of the first man and woman is found in Genesis, the first book in the Bible. In the third chapter, it tells about God making Adam and Eve and placing them in the beautiful Garden of Eden that he prepared for them. They were to care for it and enjoy its wonderful fruit. There was only one tree in the whole garden that God forbade Adam and Eve to eat from — the tree of the knowledge of good and evil. They were very happy in the Garden of Eden** *(EVE bobs up, humming softly but clearly)* **until one day a stranger intruded.**

SERPENT: *(Bobs up at other end of stage, standing high, with head level, toward the audience.)* **He-he-he, doesn't she seem happy! I'll soon put a stop to that.** *(Moves toward EVE.)* **Good morning, Eve.**

EVE: **Good Morning. I don't believe I ever saw you in our garden before.**

SERPENT: **I'm just strolling through. Did God say you couldn't eat any of the fruit in the garden?**

EVE: **Oh, no! God said we could eat anything we want except for the fruit of that one tree.** *(Points)* **We aren't even supposed to touch it, lest we die!**

SERPENT: **You won't die! God knows that your eyes will**

be opened and you will be as wise as God if you eat
that fruit. God doesn't want you to be wise like he is!

EVE: *(Turning to look at tree and touching the fruit)* **It does look
good. And I would love to be wise like God.** *(Considers
for a moment, then takes and appears to eat.)* **Mmmm, this
is good. I must tell Adam about it. Adam! Adam!**

SERPENT: **He-he-he.** *(Exits at one end as ADAM enters on
other end.)*

EVE: **Taste this fruit, Adam. It's really delicious.**
(Continues as ADAM begins to shake his head.) **The serpent
said that we wouldn't die and that it would make us
wise. Come on, wouldn't you like to be wise?**

ADAM: *(Slowly takes fruit and tastes.)* **It is good.** *(Eats more.
Then suddenly he throws down the fruit.)* **I feel awful, Eve!
We have disobeyed God! The serpent tricked us into
disobeying God! Quick, let's hide before God comes
to visit us. He will be very angry!**

VOICE: **Adam! Adam!**

ADAM: **That's God's voice! Quick, we must hide!** *(Both
duck out.)*

VOICE: **Adam! Where are you, Adam?** *(ADAM and EVE
reluctantly appear.)* **Where have you been, Adam?**

ADAM: **We heard your voice and we hid. We are naked and
we didn't want you to see us that way.**

VOICE: **Who told you that you were naked? Have you eaten
of the tree that I told you not to eat of?**

ADAM: **The woman that you gave to be with me ate some
of the fruit and gave some to me to eat.**

VOICE: **Eve, what have you done?**

EVE: **The serpent deceived me. He told me that we wouldn't
die and that it would make us wise.**

VOICE: **Serpent!** *(SERPENT bobs up.)* **You are cursed above
all cattle and beasts because you have done this. On
your belly shall you go and dust shall you eat all the
days of your life. And from this day forward you and
mankind shall be bitter enemies.** *(SERPENT falls down
low and slinks out.)* **Eve, you shall bear children in sorrow
and your husband shall rule over you. And Adam,
because you listened to the voice of your wife, you both
shall be driven from this beautiful garden. From now**

on you shall plow the ground — which will be cursed
with thorns and thistles — and will earn your food by
the sweat of your brow. You are made out of dirt. Death
has already begun in your body and you will eventually
die and your body will go back to the dust from which
it was made. *(ADAM and EVE bow their heads and slowly
exit.)*

ANNOUNCER: Listening to the voice of the old serpent,
who was the devil, caused Adam and Eve to lose their
lovely home. Did you know he is still deceiving people
today? Has he told you that you want to have fun now
and will come to God later, or that you are so good you
don't need to accept Christ, or some other lie? God's
Word says: "Today is the day of salvation." Let us not
put off accepting Jesus as our savior. We have no
promise of tomorrow. Let's give our hearts to him right
now.

A Foolish Young Man

Puppets: NOAH, YOUNG MAN, WIFE, MINISTER, SCIENTIST
(NOAH moves onto stage with hammer in hand. Hammer may be secured to part of a movable arm and hand with wire or a heavy rubber band. Begins to hammer. YOUNG MAN enters from the other end of stage.)

YOUNG MAN: **Say there, old man, what is that strange thing you are building?**

NOAH: **I'm building a boat.**

YOUNG MAN: **A boat? Way up here on the hillside? How will you get it down to the river?**

NOAH: **I'm not building it to float on the river. A great flood is coming on the earth and I plan to save myself and my family in this ark.**

YOUNG MAN: **How do you know this?**

NOAH: **God told me. God told me how to build this boat and he said that rain would fall from the heavens and cover the whole earth.**

YOUNG MAN: **Ha-ha-ha. Who ever heard of such a thing? Water covering the whole earth. Ha-ha-ha. I think you're crazy.**

NOAH: **A flood is coming whether you believe it or not. God said so and I believe God! Every living thing that is not in this ark will be killed by the waters.**

YOUNG MAN: *(Scoffingly)* **Why would God destroy the people he made?**

NOAH: **Because man has become so wicked and violent. Man has become so bad that God is sorry he ever made man.**

YOUNG MAN: **Why did God warn you so you could escape?**

NOAH: **Because I serve God and try to please him.**

YOUNG MAN: *(Thoughtfully)* **How could I be saved?**

NOAH: **If you will turn away from your wicked ways and help us build the ark, I'm sure God will save you too.**

YOUNG MAN: **I'll go talk to my wife about it right now. And I'll see you later.**

NOAH: **We'll be glad to have you join us. But don't wait too long.** *(Both exit.)*

(Play a verse or so of music to show time elapse.)

YOUNG MAN: *(Coming on stage)* **Wife! Wife!** *(WIFE appears.)* **Oh, there you are. Say, we don't have a minute to lose if we want to be saved! There's a man out on the hillside building a big boat and he said —**

WIFE: *(Interrupting)* **I know what he said. You've been listening to that crazy old man, Noah.** *(Mockingly)* **And he said there's a flood coming out of the sky and everyone who doesn't get in his silly old boat will be drowned!**

YOUNG MAN: **Don't you believe his story?**

WIFE: **No, I don't! When I was a little girl he was building that ark and preaching that a flood was coming. And a flood hasn't come yet!**

YOUNG MAN: **But — but he seemed so sincere and I felt down in my heart that God had spoken to him. What if Noah *is* right and we are all drowned because we don't believe.**

WIFE: **I'll tell you what. Go talk to our pastor and see what he says.**

YOUNG MAN: **That's a good idea! I'll go right now.**
(Musical interlude)
(MINISTER enters. A knock is heard. MINISTER moves to other end of stage and appears to open door.)

MINISTER: **Come in, my boy, come in! What can I do for you?**

YOUNG MAN: *(Entering)* **I've been talking to Noah. Do you believe God is really going to destroy the people of the earth with a flood because we are so wicked?**

MINISTER: **Ha-ha-ha. Of course not! That old man is a fanatic — just an old kill-joy. People aren't really so bad. I say, "let's eat, drink and be merry!" Forget about old Noah! You're too young to worry about dying. Have a good time and let the future take care of itself!**

YOUNG MAN: *(Doubtfully)* **Well — OK — if you say so. I guess you should know.** *(Exits.)*
(Musical interlude)

NARRATOR: **It is a few days later.** *(YOUNG MAN and SCIENTIST enter together.)*

YOUNG MAN: *(Looking toward other end of the stage)* **What in the world is happening over there by Noah's ark?**

SCIENTIST: **A bunch of animals are going into Noah's boat.**

YOUNG MAN: *(Excitedly)* **Then Noah's story is true! And even the animals believe a flood is coming.**

SCIENTIST: **Don't get excited, young man. I'm a scientist and I'm sure there is a logical explanation why pairs of animals would file into the ark this way. I've come to study them and discover why.**

YOUNG MAN: **I believe Noah is telling the truth! It may begin to rain any minute! I'm going home and get my wife and get in Noah's ark before it's too late.**

SCIENTIST: **Do you want people laughing and making fun of you like they do at Noah and his family?**

YOUNG MAN: **I'd rather be laughed at than drown!** *(Turns and walks rapidly away.)*

SCIENTIST: *(Shaking his head as he watches him go)* **Tut-tut. Poor, ignorant soul.** *(Exits)*

NARRATOR: **It's a few minutes later.**

YOUNG MAN: *(Rushing onto the stage out of breath)* **Wife — wife!** *(She enters.)* **Come quick! We've got to get in Noah's ark! Animals — a male and female of each kind — are filing into the ark right now. It could start raining at any minute!**

WIFE: *(Angrily)* **I've had enough of this foolishness! I'll not leave my nice home and go live with a bunch of wild animals and be laughed at! Besides, Noah would think the things I like to do are sinful, and I don't plan to quit doing them for anyone!**

YOUNG MAN: **But, Wife, we may drown if —**

WIFE: **Not another word! I'd rather drown than go live with the "holy" preacher and his family! And if you say another word about it, I . . . I'll go home to mother!**

YOUNG MAN: *(Sadly)* **Yes, dear. But I have the feeling that is just what we will do — drown!** *(Both exit, WIFE flouncing out, YOUNG MAN more slowly, with bowed head.)*

NARRATOR: **The foolish young man was right. After the animals and Noah's family were in the boat, God shut the door. After seven days, a terrible flood came on the earth — just as Noah had said — and everyone on the whole earth that was not in the ark was drowned.**

     The Bible says that Jesus is coming back to the earth to take his people home with him. Some people

laugh, just as they did in Noah's day, but Jesus is coming back whether people believe it or not. The only ones who are going with him are the ones who have invited Christ into their hearts and are living for God. Are you ready to go? Jesus is the big boat and all who are not on his boat will not go. Are you in the Jesus boat? If not, you can be.

Man Overboard

Puppets: JONAH, CAPTAIN, SAILOR

NARRATOR: *(Use a whale puppet if one is available.)* **I am Jonah, a killer whale. I took that name because many years ago one of my ancestors swallowed a man by the name of Jonah. Don't laugh, he really did! I expect he had a bellyache! Here's how it all happened:**

Many years ago a Jewish prophet named Jonah was given a mission by God. God told Jonah, "Go to the wicked people of Nineveh and tell them that in forty days I shall destroy their city because of their evil ways." But Jonah did not want to obey God. *(WHALE/ NARRATOR exits and JONAH appears on stage.)*

JONAH: **I don't like the people of Nineveh. They are the enemies of my people. If I go preach to them, they might stop doing bad things and turn to God. Then God would not destroy them because he is so kind.**

They're our enemies, why should I warn them? I'm not going to Nineveh! I'll catch a boat and go far away from here. I'll go to Tarshish — that's what I'll do! *(Exits)*

NARRATOR: *(WHALE appears or voice of NARRATOR is heard.)* **So Jonah ran away from God — or tried to anyway. He bought a ticket and got on a boat to Tarshish. He felt very proud of himself. But God, who sees everything, knew right where he was. And God sent a terrible storm and began to rock the boat about. Everyone was scared to death except Jonah. He had gone down into the hold of the boat and was sound asleep.** *(CAPTAIN and SAILOR enter. Both should sway as if having difficulty standing because of the storm.)*

CAPTAIN: **This is a terrible storm. Have you had the men throw the cargo overboard?**

SAILOR: **Yes, sir, but the ship is still in danger of being swamped by the waves. I'm afraid we are all going to be drowned!**

CAPTAIN: **Have all the sailors pray to their gods that our lives will be saved!**

SAILOR: **The sailors are already praying, sir. They know**

unless something happens soon the ship is going to be
smashed by the waves and we will all be lost!

CAPTAIN: Make a list of the sailors' names. We'll cast
lots and find out which man's god is angry with him
and causing this storm.

SAILOR: Yes, sir! Do I add the passenger's name?

CAPTAIN: Yes, certainly! By the way, where is that
passenger?

SAILOR: He's down inside the ship asleep.

CAPTAIN: Get that list made while I go talk to our
passenger.

SAILOR: Yes, sir! *(Exits)*

CAPTAIN: *(Goes to other end of stage, looks down and calls
loudly.)* Jonah! Jonah! Wake up! There is an awful storm
upon us! Cry aloud to your God that we will be saved!

JONAH: *(Appears, swaying and rubbing his eyes.)* What did
you say? A storm?

CAPTAIN: Yes, you foolish man, a storm! How you can
sleep during a storm like this is more than I know!

SAILOR: *(Rushing in)* Captain, Captain! We drew lots and
the lot fell upon that passenger. He is the cause of the
storm!

CAPTAIN: *(Turning back to JONAH)* Are you the one who
has caused this storm by doing something to displease
your God?

JONAH: Yes, I have done a very bad thing. I have not
obeyed my God.

CAPTAIN: This is very serious! Where do you come from?
What do you do for a living? And what evil things have
you done to cause this storm?

JONAH: I am a Jewish prophet from the land of Israel. I
serve the true God — the almighty, living God who
made the heavens and the earth. My God sent me to
the city of Nineveh to preach against it, but I didn't
want to go and ran away from God. He sent this storm
because of me.

CAPTAIN: What can we do to get him to stop the storm?

JONAH: Throw me overboard!

CAPTAIN: We don't want to do that! *(Yells)* Men! Row hard!
Row hard! *(CAPTAIN, SAILOR and JONAH sway violently.)*

SAILOR: **Sir, the waves are about to smash the boat and we will all die! What can we do?**

CAPTAIN: **There is only one thing we can do and I pray Jonah's God will forgive us. We must throw Jonah overboard.** *(CAPTAIN and SAILOR pick up JONAH and swing him. The head of the WHALE appears with wide open mouth and JONAH falls into it and the head sinks with him in its jaw. If no WHALE is available, have JONAH thrown over and disappearing. The other two men exit.)*

NARRATOR: **As soon as Jonah was thrown overboard, the sea became calm. After the huge fish swallowed Jonah, it went down-down-down. This was a special fish prepared by God. Jonah was in the belly of the whale for three days. He was very frightened and he prayed to God.** *(If available, drop down thin curtain with WHALE painted on it. Bring small JONAH puppet up behind curtain so it appears JONAH is inside WHALE.)*

JONAH: *(Running here and there seeking an escape hatch. Finally stops and speaks to himself.)* **This is terrible! I have searched and searched and there is no way out of this fish. I'm going to die and it will serve me right! I should have known better than to disobey God. If only I had gone to preach to those sinners as God told me to! I would go in a minute if God would give me another chance! I'm going to pray. God saw me running away from him on that ship so he can surely see me down in this smelly old fish.** *(He kneels.)*

Heavenly Father, I've been a very foolish man. I'm sorry I didn't go preach as you asked. If you'll get me out of this fish, I promise to go right away to Nineveh and preach your message. *(He is quickly moved across stage and out as if he is being thrust out of WHALE's mouth. Curtain is drawn up as NARRATOR begins to speak.)*

NARRATOR: **God was good to Jonah and gave him another chance. He commanded the huge fish to bring Jonah to the top of the waters and spit him out on the shore. As soon as he landed on dry ground, Jonah ran as fast as he could to Nineveh and began to preach:**

JONAH'S VOICE: **In forty days God is going to destroy Nineveh. Because you are wicked, evil people, God is**

going to kill you all. Hear ye! Hear ye! You have only forty more days to live because God is going to kill you all because of your sinful, mean ways. Hear ye, all ye Ninevites, in forty days God will destroy your city.

NARRATOR: The people of Nineveh believed Jonah and fasted and prayed and turned away from their sinful, wicked ways. This is the reason God wanted Jonah to preach to them, so they would have a chance to turn to God and away from their evil ways. God was merciful and allowed them to live. He is still merciful today and wants everyone to turn to him and away from sin. Will you believe, like the Ninevites did, and ask God to forgive your sins?

CHAPTER 6

Church Life Plays

- Excuses! Excuses!
- Mister Grump
- Happy Jack Attends Church
- Ralphie Moves

Excuses! Excuses!

Puppets: CROAKY, a frog; SHEP, a dog; and MARCY, a girl.

CROAKY: *(Appears sputtering and coughing.)* **A fellow can't have a bit of peace anymore!** *(Coughs)* **Not a bit of peace!**

SHEP: *(Appearing)* **Hey, Croaky, what happened to you?**

CROAKY: *(Coughs)* **I nearly strangled to death, that's what! Marshy Pond's been invaded by motor boats! The big waves they stirred up washed me clear off my lily pad and nearly choked me to death!** *(Coughs)*

SHEP: **That's too bad, old friend. Are you OK now?**

CROAKY: **I'll survive, I guess. What are *you* doing this bright Sunday morning?**

SHEP: **I was coming down to see you. The Browns, the humans I live with, have all gone to Sunday school. They left early because Mr. Brown was taking a whole carload of people to church today.**

CROAKY: *(Grumbling)* **I wish all those boaters had gone to church! I heard one of them say it was too pretty a day to spend in church.**

SHEP: **Mr. Brown says that's just an excuse. He said if it was raining the same people would say it was too wet — or too cold — or too hot. All just excuses!**

CROAKY: **Yeah, humans sure don't realize how fortunate they are. God's son died on the cross for them, so they could go to heaven, and they spend their Sundays fishing, boating or picnicking instead of going to church and thanking God. Wish I was a human. I'd go to church every Sunday!**

SHEP: **Me too! I always wanted to go to church. I tried to get in the church this morning but they chased me out. They said,** *(In mimicking voice)* **"Dogs don't belong in church."** *(Pauses, then speaks excitedly.)* **But do you know what I saw there?**

CROAKY: **No, what?**

SHEP: **A goat! Can you imagine that?**

CROAKY: **No, I sure can't! They let a goat come to church but wouldn't let you? What's going on?**

SHEP: **The Sunday school superintendent brought him for the kids to pet and the kids have been coming in droves**

to church. Even the adults are crazy about that silly little goat! Imagine! Crazy about a goat! *(Shakes his head in disgust.)* I never can figure humans out.

CROAKY: Me neither! Say, here comes Marcy.

MARCY: *(Coming toward them)* Hello, Croaky, Hi, Shep.

SHEP: Where are you going all dressed up?

MARCY: I'm going to Sunday school. We always have lots of fun, but the past two Sundays our Sunday school superintendent has been bringing a darling little goat for us to play with!

SHEP: *(Speaks over his shoulder to CROAKY.)* See what I mean? You can never figure humans out! Who ever heard of a "darling" goat?

CROAKY: You mean you really *enjoy* going to church?

MARCY: Oh, yes! We sing and hear stories and learn about God. It's really great!

CROAKY: Apparently everyone doesn't think it's fun. This morning I overheard a man in a motorboat telling another man he never wanted to go to church again because he had to go when he was a kid.

MARCY: I don't know what church that man went to, but our church is so much fun, I look forward to going all week long.

SHEP: My master, Mr. Brown, says that most reasons people give for not going to church are really just excuses. He said some people say they are too sick to go to church — but they're not too sick to go for a drive or even to work. He said some even use the excuse that they don't have clothes to wear to church.

CROAKY: Do you have to wear special clothes to church?

MARCY: Of course not! Most people wear their best clothes to church because it's God's house, but our church people make everyone welcome, even if they aren't wearing nice clothes!

SHEP: Our neighbor has more excuses for not going to church than a hound dog has fleas. He invents a brand new one every time Mr. Brown invites him to church. He's too tired, or he's waiting for a phone call, or he has company coming.

MARCY: That sounds like our neighbor. When mother invited him to church, he said they had to keep their little boy in because he had a cold. But we saw them all get in the car before we had gone a block and they didn't come home until late that night.

CROAKY: You mean humans lie about why they don't go to church?!

SHEP: Sometimes, I think they even lie to themselves. But sometimes they run out of made-up excuses and even tell the truth. Once when Mr. Brown invited our neighbor to prayer meeting, he just out and told the truth. He said *Incredible Hulk* was on TV that night and he didn't want to miss it.

MARCY: Those poor people don't know what they're missing in church! I feel sorry for them. I'd better go now, I don't want to be late. I sure hope I get to pet that cute little goat again today! Bye, fellows. *(Exits)*

SHEP: They sure do have lots of fun down at that church! Wish I could go! Say! Maybe I could glue some horns on my head and they'd think I was a goat. Then they'd let *me* in!

CROAKY: Sorry, old buddy. You would only look like a dog with horns. We're not humans and they won't let us in.

SHEP: Yeah, you're right. But I still think humans have all the fun.

Mister Grump

Puppets: MARCY, MISTER GRUMP
(MARCY and MISTER GRUMP enter at each end of stage.)

GRUMP: Good morning, Marcy. Where are you going so early this Sunday morning?

MARCY: Hi, Mister Grump. I'm on my way to church. Why don't you come with me?

GRUMP: Not me! My mother *made* me go to church all the time when I was a kid, so I made up my mind to never go to church again when I got away from home. And I haven't!

MARCY: My church is so much fun, Mother doesn't have to make me go.

GRUMP: Fun? I'll bet! Anybody knows when you start goin' to church you can't have any fun anymore. Don't do this! Don't do that! Isn't that right?

MARCY: Well — I know Christians aren't to do *some* things, but our pastor says the Christian life is a practical life. God never asks us to quit *anything* unless it isn't good for us.

GRUMP: Yep! Just what I thought! You can't have any fun!

MARCY: The people of our church do all kinds of fun things together. And when someone has a problem or trouble, everyone is concerned and tries to help. But best of all, we can talk to God and he helps us.

GRUMP: I know some of the people in your church, and that George White is just a hypocrite!

MARCY: There could be some hypocrites in my church, I don't know. But if there are, we have so many good people that we shouldn't worry about the bad apples.

GRUMP: I wouldn't go to church with a hypocrite like that George White!

MARCY: Our pastor says if we let hypocrites stand between us and God that they are closer to God than we are.

GRUMP: Huh, huh.

MARCY: I think you would like our pastor. His sermons are so interesting that even us kids like to hear him. I sure wish you would come with me.

GRUMP: Hummm — what time does church start?

MARCY: Sunday school starts at nine-thirty and church at ten-thirty.

GRUMP: I don't think I could swallow Sunday school but I could go to regular church. Your preacher sounds like he might make some sense. So I'll see you at ten-thirty.

MARCY: Wonderful! I'll watch for you. Bye now. *(Exits)*

GRUMP: (Watching her go) **That kid *really* seems to like church. I gotta find out why. Could it be that I've been wrong all these years and was lookin' for only the bad? Well, I'll give it a try. I hope the church roof doesn't fall in or the people faint when they see me comin'!** *(Exits)*

Happy Jack Attends Church

One PUPPET and one live TEACHER needed.
(TEACHER is leading a children's service when HAPPY JACK appears on puppet stage.)
HAPPY JACK: May I stay and listen?
TEACHER: OK, Happy Jack, you can stay if you'll be good. This is a church service.
HAPPY JACK: I'll be real good.
TEACHER: I'm going to tell you a story now, children.
(HAPPY JACK pulls out a snake — [use a bright-colored toy snake] — and begins to play with it. TEACHER notices.)
Happy Jack, you are not supposed to bring snakes to church. It's a very special place. So put him away or you'll have to leave.
HAPPY JACK: Oh, all right, but she wouldn't hurt anyone. She's a pet — see . . . . *(Holds snake out toward TEACHER.)*
TEACHER: *(Draws away in alarm.)* Happy Jack!
HAPPY JACK: OK. *(Puts snake away. TEACHER turns away and he pulls out a big black bug — [use a plastic one] — to play with.)*
TEACHER: *(Sees the bug.)* Happy Jack! I told you we can't bring things like that to church!
HAPPY JACK: You said to not play with snakes in church. This isn't a snake, it's my pet beetle.
TEACHER: Now, Happy Jack, you'll just have to leave. We can't have your pets disturbing the service. Church is God's house and we don't bring things like that to church.
HAPPY JACK: Please let me stay. I promise to put my pets in my pocket and be *real* good. Cross my heart and hope to die.
TEACHER: You don't have to be that drastic. And you can stay if you behave yourself. If you don't, out you go.
HAPPY JACK: OK.
TEACHER: *(Turns back to class.)* Now, class, as I was saying, I'm going to tell you a story. *(HAPPY JACK begins to hum as soon as she starts to speak and then to whistle. Turns to HAPPY JACK and speaks sternly.)* **Happy Jack, you**

promised to be good and now you're whistling.

HAPPY JACK: It's a church song.

TEACHER: Out you go! You'll teach these kids bad habits.

HAPPY JACK: I'm just a little puppet. How was I to know?

TEACHER: Puppet or not, I think it will do you good to go home and think about how you are supposed to act in church.

HAPPY JACK: Well, OK . . . . *(Exits reluctantly.)*

Ralphie Moves

Two Puppets: RALPHIE, a church mouse; SHEP, a dog
(RALPHIE enters, with knapsack over his shoulder, walking fast.)

SHEP: *(Entering)* **Hey there, Ralphie, where are you going in such a hurry?**

RALPHIE: **Oh, hi, Shep. I'm moving.**

SHEP: **Moving? I thought you liked living in a church. You're always calling yourself a church mouse.**

RALPHIE: **I do like living in a church, and especially that one.** *(Indicates with motion of his head.)* **I was born there and have lived there all my life.**

SHEP: **Why are you leaving, then?**

RALPHIE: **I'm just plain disgusted with the people who attend church over there!**

SHEP: **Yeah? What's wrong with them?**

RALPHIE: **Did you ever attend church services?**

SHEP: **Naw, the Browns — the people I live with — think dogs shouldn't go in a church. Mr. Brown says dogs don't know how to act in church and would disturb everyone.**

RALPHIE: **If your master thinks dogs don't know how to act, he should see how some of the people in my church act, especially the kids!**

SHEP: **How do they act?**

RALPHIE: **I don't want to talk about it! It gives me a headache to even think about it.**

SHEP: **Aw, come on, what do the people do that have you so upset?**

RALPHIE: **I can't talk about it.**

SHEP: **Come on — tell me about it.**

RALPHIE: **Oh, all right. I'll just tell you about last night's service. That'll give you an idea of what goes on.**

SHEP: **I'm all ears.**

RALPHIE: **Well, from the beginning of the service the kids, and even a few of the grown-ups, just wouldn't stay put in their seats. Some of them went to the bathroom or to get a drink at least a half dozen times, I know.**

SHEP: **Maybe they needed to.**

RALPHIE: Baloney! And some of them kept changing
    seats. You'd have thought they were jumping beans!
SHEP: And Mr. Brown said a dog would disturb everyone.
RALPHIE: Yeah! It was disgraceful! Some people wanted to
    listen to the pastor preach but the others kept
    whispering and giggling and changing seats. Pretty
    soon everyone about gave up trying to hear the pastor.
SHEP: What did the pastor do?
RALPHIE: He asked everyone to settle down two or three
    times but they didn't pay any attention to him. Do you
    know, Shep, that some of those kids even brought
    candy and gum and sunflower seeds to church! Between
    paper a-crackling, shells a-popping and gum a-
    smacking, you'd have thought you were at a circus.
SHEP: Say! Maybe I could sneak in next time if they have
    all those goodies to eat! Did they have popcorn, too?
RALPHIE: Shep! You sound as bad as those kids! You
    aren't supposed to go to church to *eat!*
SHEP: It sounds like some *people* go to church to eat —
    and play. With all that running in and out and eating,
    they probably wouldn't even notice me if I sneaked in
    real quiet. I always did want to go to church.
RALPHIE: Then that's the church to go to! They would
    never notice you in all that confusion. But I like order
    when I go to church, so that's why I'm leaving — today!
SHEP: How are people supposed to act in church?
RALPHIE: You sure *are* a dumb dog!
SHEP: The only way to get smart is to ask questions.
RALPHIE: I suppose so. OK, I'll tell you how people are
    supposed to act in church. They are supposed to choose
    a seat and sit there the whole service. They are
    supposed to get a drink and go to the bathroom *before*
    the service begins. They should stand *only* when the
    pastor or leader asks them to and should sit quietly
    and listen to what the pastor has to say. They are not
    supposed to eat, talk, giggle, whisper, or move around.
SHEP: That makes sense to me.
RALPHIE: Of course it makes sense! And I'm plumb
    ashamed of the people in my church, so I'm leaving!
SHEP: Aw, Ralphie, why don't you give them another chance?

RALPHIE: Nope! I've had it clear up to my Adam's apple. I'm finding me another church! I'll see you when I get settled. So long. *(Turns away.)*

SHEP: Goodbye, Ralphie. *(Watches RALPHIE go and sadly shakes his head.)* I wonder how many *people* have left that church for the very same reason Ralphie is leaving. Too bad — too bad . . . . *(Exits slowly, shaking his head.)*

CHAPTER 7

Christian Behavior Plays

- A Lesson in Health
- Temper! Temper!
- That's a Lie, Jimmy!
- That's Stealing!
- A Quarrel
- Sharing
- Twenty Dollar Bill
- Real Love
- Where's That Pin?
- Mean Ole Gert

A Lesson on Health

Puppets: RALPHIE, a church mouse; CROAKY, a frog.
   (RALPHIE and CROAKY enter.)

RALPHIE: Hello there! I don't think I know you.

CROAKY: My name's Croaky. What's yours?

RALPHIE: I'm Ralphie. I live in the attic of that church over there.

CROAKY: Oh — a church mouse. Wha'cha doin' down here at Marshy Pond? I didn't think mice liked water.

RALPHIE: I don't, but I like to take a stroll down here next to the water sometimes. The air is so fresh and clean, not full of cigarette smoke and car fumes like in town.

CROAKY: Cigarette smoke? What's that?

RALPHIE: You mean you never saw a cigarette?

CROAKY: Not that I know of.

RALPHIE: Well, you haven't missed anything. It's one of those things humans use to ruin the healthy bodies God gave them. Anyway, I'll tell you about cigarettes. They're little sticks made out of tobacco rolled up tight in little pieces of paper. A human sticks one end in his mouth and sets the other end on fire.

CROAKY: *(Chuckling)* You would probably burn off your whiskers if you tried that.

RALPHIE: Yeah! I'm not stupid enough to try it. But the truth is that it doesn't burn them. They just puff smoke out all over the place. It stings everyone's nose and eyes.

CROAKY: But why do humans use cigarettes if they are so awful?

RALPHIE: I guess it makes them feel good while they do it. But I heard a preacher say in church the other day that cigarettes slowly ruin tobacco smokers' lungs and also causes them to get cancer, heart trouble and other bad diseases that they can die from.

CROAKY: Don't people know tobacco hurts them?

RALPHIE: Sure! It says on the package that tobacco could hurt them. But humans must not be smart like us animals.

CROAKY: *(Shaking his head sadly)* **Apparently not.**

RALPHIE: **Do you know that some people use an even worse kind of cigarette?**

CROAKY: *(Shocked)* **No! What kind is that?**

RALPHIE: **It's made out of marijuana. It's called "grass" by some, but it isn't the good kind of grass like we have in the fields around here. This marijuana kind of grass makes humans crazy and they do weird things, like a drunk person.**

CROAKY: **Drunk?**

RALPHIE: **Yeah, drunk. You've sure lived a sheltered life in this pond if you never saw a drunk person. Drinking wine, whiskey and beer makes a person drunk. They can't walk or think straight so they have car wrecks and get into all kinds of trouble.**

CROAKY: **My, my! How awful!**

RALPHIE: **You can say that again! There's some drugs a human can use that can ruin their minds forever — LSD and heroin are two of them. Some are pills that a person can swallow and some kinds are put into the arm with a big needle and some are sniffed up the nose. But all of it can make a human crazy.**

CROAKY: **But how can humans be so dumb as to use such things?**

RALPHIE: **They say it makes them feel good for a while. But I don't need anything to make me feel good, do you?**

CROAKY: **Of course not! God gave me a good healthy body, nice water to swim in, the sun to warm me and lots of food to eat, so I feel good without those drugs, cigarettes and other stuff.**

RALPHIE: **Me, too! Could it be that animals are just smarter than humans? You never see animals puffing out smoke or sticking needles of dope in their arms or drinking alcohol so they can't think straight!**

CROAKY: **How right you are! I guess we should feel sorry for those poor dumb humans.**

RALPHIE: **But not all humans are like that. There's some smart ones left. Some of them attend the church where I live. They're called Christians, and they never use those harmful things. You know, they are the happiest** people, and can they ever sing! Sometimes they make me wish I was a human. But if I was a human, I'd want to be a Christian human!

Temper! Temper!

Puppets: GRANDMA; and granddaughter, MARCY
   (GRANDMA comes in at end of stage. A knock is heard.)
GRANDMA: *(Calls)* **Come in.** *(MARCY enters.)* **Come on in,
   Marcy. Would you like a cookie?**
MARCY: *(Head low)* **No, thank you.**
GRANDMA: **It's very hot today, isn't it?**
MARCY: **Uh-huh.**
GRANDMA: **What's wrong, dear?**
MARCY: **Nothing.**
GRANDMA: **I know something's wrong when my grand-
   daughter won't eat a cookie.**
MARCY: **Boo-hoo-hoo. Grandma, I'm so ashamed of
   myself! Boo-hoo-hoo!**
GRANDMA: **What's wrong, dear? It can't be** *that* **bad!**
MARCH: **Oh, Grandma, it is! It is! I don't think I can ever
   talk about it!**
GRANDMA: **Can't you tell me, dear?** *(MARCY shakes her
   head "no".)* **Then you can tell Jesus about it. He loves
   you.**
MARCY: **Boo-hoo-hoo. No, he doesn't love me anymore!
   I can't talk to him!**
GRANDMA: **What is it? You must talk to someone. What
   happened?**
MARCY: **I'm so ashamed! Tommie was teasing me at
   school and he wouldn't stop. I got madder and madder
   and he just teased me that much more. Then I started
   to yell and scream at him. I — I just couldn't hold my
   temper.**
GRANDMA: **You really let your temper get away, didn't you?**
MARCY: **Yes, I did. And I said a bad word and even used
   God's name as a swear word! So I can't ever talk to
   Jesus again! Boo-hoo-hoo!**
GRANDMA: **Gracious, child, it's true you did a very bad
   thing but you can still talk to Jesus about it. He . . . .**
MARCY: **No, I can't! And it's all Tommie's fault! Boo-hoo-hoo.**
GRANDMA: **Calm down, dear, and stop crying so we can
   talk about it.**
MARCY: **You're not mad at me?**

GRANDMA: Of course not! Now, let's get some things straight. First of all, you can't go through life blaming Tommie — or anyone — for your wrong-doing.

MARCY: But, Grandma . . . .

GRANDMA: Listen, Marcy. If you sin, no one *made* you sin. Tommie teased you and upset you, but it was you who lost your temper. And remember, child, that when we need help, God will help us, if we ask him. God can help us overcome any bad habit.

MARCY: But will God ever forgive me for losing my temper and yelling and using his name in vain?

GRANDMA: Of course he will! You did a bad thing, but the Bible says if we ask him to forgive us, he will.

MARCY: *(Relieved)* Oh, I'm so glad! I'm going to ask Jesus to forgive me and help me to not lose my temper again.

GRANDMA: You are a wise little girl and I'm sure God will help you. *(Pauses)* Marcy, do you pray each morning and ask God to be with you throughout the day?

MARCY: Oh, yes! But this morning we got up late and I didn't have time to pray.

GRANDMA: Don't you know you can pray on the way to school, or when you are eating, or standing in line, or anywhere?

MARCY: How can I do that?

GRANDMA: The Bible tells us to pray without ceasing. That means we can pray in our hearts as we go about our work or play. That keeps us in touch with God all the time.

MARCY: That's what I'm going to do! Then when I'm tempted to lose my temper again or to do something else bad, I'll know God is right there with me to help.

GRANDMA: That's how to live a happy and successful life, Marcy.

MARCY: Jesus is really a good friend and so are you, Grandma! And now will you pray with me? I want to ask God to forgive me for losing my temper. Then I think I'll eat that cookie you were going to give me.

GRANDMA: I'll have one, too. Let's pray. *(Both bow their heads and sink from sight.)*

That's a Lie, Jimmy!

Puppets: JIMMY and SAMMY, two boy puppets; MOTHER, a lady puppet (or a grandmother could be substituted for mother).

NARRATOR: School has just let out. Jimmy is waiting in front of his house for his friend, Paul. They are going swimming.

JIMMY: *(Appears)* Yippee! School's out for three whole months! Am I ever going to have fun! Boy, oh boy, oh boy! *(Goes over to edge of stage and appears to be looking down the street.)* I wonder what's keeping Paul. He said he'd be here at nine o'clock to go swimming. I can hardly wait to get into that cool, cool water! *(Leans out over stage edge to look again.)* I sure wish Paul would hurry! Uh-oh, there comes that new kid from down the street. I sure don't want him tagging along. I'll pretend I don't see him. *(Turns around and begins to hum or whistle softly.)*

SAMMY: Hello, Jimmy. I saw Paul yesterday and he said you two were going swimming. Can I come, too?

JIMMY: *(Turning back around)* Hi, Sammy, I didn't see you coming by. Uh — uh — we were going swimming this morning but Paul called awhile ago and said he had to go to the dentist.

SAMMY: Well, OK. But couldn't we go by ourselves?

JIMMY: Not this morning. I'm really too busy to go right now.

SAMMY: *(Turning away)* Oh. Well, I'll be seeing you. *(Exits)*

JIMMY: I got rid of that pest! I sure wish Paul would hurry.

MOTHER: *(Appears)* Jimmy, did I hear you tell Sammy just now that you weren't going swimming? I thought you were going with Paul.

JIMMY: Uh — uh — Paul can't come right now. He has to help his mother for a while.

MOTHER: Good, then you can work for a while cleaning out the garage.

JIMMY: *(Acting as if he is in pain)* I really don't feel so good. My stomach hurts.

MOTHER: It does? Then you had better come in the house and go to bed.

JIMMY: I don't feel *that* bad. I'll just sit here in the sun and

I'm sure it will be OK in a little bit. It feels better already.

MOTHER: Young man, you come in the house this minute. If your stomach hurts you must take some medicine. A good dose of castor oil will fix it right up.

JIMMY: My stomach doesn't hurt a bit now, honest.

MOTHER: It didn't hurt to begin with, did it?

JIMMY: *(Hanging head)* No, ma'am.

MOTHER: And what about Paul having to help his mother — or did he go to the dentist, as you told Sammy? Those were lies too, weren't they?

JIMMY: Oh, no, not lies, just little fibs! Everybody tells little fibs now and then.

MOTHER: Tell me what a little fib is.

JIMMY: Well — it's something that isn't exactly true.

MOTHER: You mean it's something that isn't true at all.

JIMMY: Well — I guess so.

MOTHER: And what is a lie?

JIMMY: It's something that isn't true. But — but there is still a difference. A fib is only a little lie, and that's not so bad.

MOTHER: Jimmy, I don't find anywhere in the Bible where it says there are little lies and big lies. But the Bible does say in Revelation that *all* liars and lots of other bad people are going to a very bad place when they leave this life.

JIMMY: *(Incredulously)* Even people who tell little lies?

MOTHER: It says there is a special place that's not as bad for people who tell little fibs.

JIMMY: The Bible doesn't really say that, does it?

MOTHER: No, Jimmy, it doesn't. If a person tells lies, whether he calls them big or little, I'm afraid the Bible considers him a liar.

JIMMY: I sure don't want to end up in that bad place. I'm going to ask God to forgive me for lying and I don't plan to tell any more lies, big or little!

MOTHER: That's a very wise choice, son. Why don't you come into the house and we'll pray together about it.

JIMMY: *(Happily)* OK, Mother. And I think I'll invite Sammy to go swimming with Paul and me, too. *(MOTHER puts her arm about JIMMY and they exit together.)*

That's Stealing!

Puppets: JACK, a boy; MARCY, a girl.

JACK: *(Enters with MARCY.)* **Boy, oh boy, oh boy! You should have been with us kids last night! We ate so much watermelon I don't think I ever want to *see* one of those things again!**

MARCY: **You sure must have got 'em cheap to get so many. What store did you get 'em from? I know Mother would like to buy some.**

JACK: **We didn't buy them. We got them from Farmer Jones' watermelon patch.**

MARCY: **You mean you *stole* the watermelons?**

JACK: **Naw — we didn't steal them. We just went out in the field and helped ourselves.**

MARCY: **That's stealing!**

JACK: **That is not stealing! Farmer Jones has a whole field full of watermelons. But he sure is stingy with them! So it was lots of fun getting them. He saw us after we had gotten a bunch, and he ran out in the field with a pitchfork, yelling, and was as mad as hops. He's so fat that he couldn't catch anyone, though! Ha-ha-ha.**

MARCY: **You should be ashamed for stealing that poor farmer's watermelons!**

JACK: **Aw, stop saying we stole them. You're just mad 'cause you didn't get in on our watermelon party!**

MARCY: **Would you think it was stealing if someone went into your backyard and picked a lot of the peaches off your dad's prize peach tree?**

JACK: **But that's different — we only have one tree and he has lots of watermelons. A whole big field of them. More than he can ever use.**

MARCY: **Happy Jack, you know that's not true! Farmer Jones raises those melons to sell. They're his living — and he worked hard out in the fields in the hot sun to raise them.**

JACK: **Aw — you make it sound so bad. He . . . .**

MARCY: *(Interrupting)* **It is bad! And it isn't right! Your father works in an office and if someone stole all his peaches, it wouldn't be all that serious, because those**

peaches aren't what buys clothes and food for your family.

JACK: (Slowly) I see what you mean. We just didn't realize, Marcy. We didn't really mean to steal — it just seemed like so much fun to grab the melons and see that fat old guy running around, chasing us with a pitchfork. It was really comical. But now I see it wasn't funny at all.

MARCY: I know you didn't really mean to steal or hurt anyone. We kids are all pretty thoughtless sometimes. What are you going to do about it?

JACK: (Thoughtfully) I'm not sure. (Is silent for a moment — in thought.) I know what! I'll get all the kids together and we'll pool our money and take it to Farmer Jones and tell him we're sorry. What do you think?

MARCY: That sounds good to me. (Both exit.)

NARRATOR: It's a few days later. (MARCY and JACK enter from each end of stage.)

JACK: Hi, Marcy! Guess what?

MARCY: What's up?

JACK: I talked to the kids about paying for the melons we took.

MARCY: What happened?

JACK: At first some of them argued with me, just like I did with you. But, in the end, they agreed that we should pay for the watermelons. We collected what we thought would pay for the melons and added a little extra. Two of us took it over to him.

MARCY: Was he real mad?

JACK: When he found out we were some of the kids who stole his watermelons, he was real mad. Even threatened to call the cops and have us put in jail.

MARCY: Wow! Then what?

JACK: Well, his wife calmed him down and got him to listen to what we had to say. We apologized and gave him the money to pay for the melons.

MARCY: Was he still mad?

JACK: At first he just stared at us like we were aliens from outer space. Then a big smile came on his face. He grabbed my hand and nearly shook it off, telling us all

the time what fine kids we were. He even had his wife
bring us a big piece of scrumptious apple pie and a big
glass of milk before he'd let us leave.

MARCY: That's great!

JACK: But the best part is that all of us felt so good about
what we did. I'll have to confess now that I didn't feel
very good about stealing those melons in the first place.

MARCY: I know what you mean. Do you remember when I
cheated on a test at school — in the fourth grade? You
were the one who yelled at me, and told me how wrong
it was. I felt as guilty as a criminal.

JACK: *(Laughing)* If I remember correctly, the girl you
copied from did so poorly on the test, you failed anyway.

MARCY: That sure didn't help my feelings, but it served
me right. I never did cheat on another test. Say, do you
want to come over and have a slice of cold watermelon?
Mother bought two this morning and they're real good.

JACK: I don't think I'll ever want another bite of watermelon
as long as I live! But thanks anyway. I'll see you around,
though.

MARCY: Sure thing! Bye now. *(Both exit.)*

A Quarrel

Characters: TEACHER, can be a puppet or a teacher standing
near the puppet stage; and two PUPPETS, one with a big nose
and one with bulging eyes — such as frog eyes. A big nose
can be made on any mouth puppet by stuffing a small piece
of plastic or cloth lightly with cotton or polyfill, placing it over
the puppet's nose, and securing it with a rubber band.
*(TEACHER leads one song, then TOBY, the puppet with a
big nose, appears.)*

TOBY: Can I sing now?

**TEACHER: Toby, I said you could sing but I'm not ready
for you yet.**

TOBY: Please, pretty please . . . .

TEACHER: Well — *(Turns to class)* **Would you like to hear
Toby sing now?** *(Most kids will want him to sing, but if not,
TEACHER should agree to let TOBY sing anyway.)* **Very well,
we'll let you sing your song now, Toby.** *(TOBY sings a
children's song. HAPPY JACK comes in before he finishes and
listens. When song is over, HAPPY JACK begins to laugh — and
laugh, nearly doubling up with mirth.)*

TOBY: *(Demands)* **What are you laughing about? Don't you
like my singing?**

HAPPY JACK: *(Trying to talk while still half laughing*)**Y — your
song was fine. It's that nose of yours. Ha-ha. You have
the funniest and biggest nose I ever saw. Ha-ha-ha.**

TOBY: *(In offended tone)* **I have a perfectly good nose. It
serves the purpose, and besides, it's part of me and I
can't help how it looks.**

**HAPPY JACK: Ha-ha-ha. I suppose not, but it sure looks
funny anyway. You could probably join a circus and
people would pay good money to see a nose like that.
Ha-ha-ha.**

**TOBY: You shut up about my nose! I may have a big nose
but at least I don't have *bug* eyes like you!**

HAPPY JACK: *(Bristling)* **What's wrong with my eyes? I
think they're pretty nice myself!**

TOBY: *(Mockingly)* **Yeah! They stick out so far I could rake
them off with a stick!**

HAPPY JACK: *(Leaning toward TOBY threateningly)* **Another**

word about my eyes and I'll give you a fat lip to match your fat nose!

TOBY: *(Dancing up and down, chanting)* **Happy's got bug eyes. Happy's got bug eyes.** *(HAPPY JACK and TOBY move together as if about to fight.)*

TEACHER: **Stop that, you two! Stop it!** *(Both stop and look at her.)* **Aren't you ashamed? That's no way to act, especially in church and before these kids. What will they think of you?**

TOBY: **He started it!**

HAPPY JACK: **He didn't have to make fun of my eyes!**

TEACHER: **Now you two tell each other you're sorry.**

HAPPY JACK: **But I'm *not* sorry about what I said about his nose. It is funny looking.**

TOBY: **No funnier than your silly looking eyes!** *(Both are almost yelling the last two lines and appear about to fight.)*

TEACHER: **Stop that this minute! The Bible says we are to be kind to each other. Is making fun of someone being kind to that person?**

TOBY: **I didn't mean to be unkind. He just made me so mad when he made fun of my nose.**

HAPPY JACK: **I guess that was mean. Toby, I'm sorry if I hurt your feelings. And you really did sing pretty.**

TOBY: **Thanks, Happy Jack, and that was mean, what I said about your eyes. I'm sorry.**

TEACHER: **It isn't easy to say you're sorry. I'm proud of both of you!** *(Both exit, shoulder to shoulder, companionably. TEACHER should comment on being kind and not making fun of others.)*

Sharing

Puppets: CROAKY, a frog; MYRTLE, a turtle.

ANNOUNCER: **Let's go for a visit to Marshy Pond and see what old Croaky is doing today, OK?**

CROAKY: *(Coming on stage, yawning)* **After that big meal of bugs I sure feel like a little nap. Think I'll just take a little snooze here in the sun on my favorite rock.** *(Puts head down and begins to snore.)*

MYRTLE: *(Comes in and moves close to CROAKY.)* **Good morning, Croaky.**

CROAKY: *(Waking with a jerk)* **Huh-huh. Oh — it's you, Myrtle. Why did you wake me up? I was having a nice nap.**

MYRTLE: **It's too sunny and pretty to sleep. Come on, let's go for a swim.**

CROAKY: **I'm to sleepy to swim. Go away and let me sleep.**

MYRTLE: **Oh, all right, you old grouch, I'll let you sleep. I guess if you're going to take a nap I'll just climb up and take one, too.**

CROAKY: **You can't take a nap here on my favorite rock. It's my rock! And besides, you snore!**

MYRTLE: *(Incensed)* **I do not snore! And that rock doesn't belong to you any more than it does to me! It's just part of the pond!**

CROAKY: **I claim it, so it belongs to me! And I don't want to be crowded, so go take your old nap someplace else!**

MYRTLE: **My, aren't *we* a big grouch! This rock is big enough for a dozen frogs and a dozen turtles so I won't be crowding you. And I *am* taking my nap right here!**

CROAKY: **I'm warning you! Get off before I shove you off!**

MYRTLE: **You aren't a gentleman! Would you hit a lady?**

CROAKY: **I didn't say I'd hit you. I said I'd shove you off if you try to steal my rock.**

MYRTLE: **Now I'm *stealing* your old rock! Of all the crazy ideas! Just try shoving me around and I'll show you what a snapping turtle can do.** *(Moves toward CROAKY with mouth wide open.)* **I'll — I'll —**

CROAKY: *(Backing away)* **Myrtle! Would you really *bite* me, your old friend?**

MYRTLE: Well, not really I guess, but you make me so mad, being stingy with that old rock!

CROAKY: You're right, Myrtle, I am being selfish with this rock. A while back Happy Jack shared his supper with me when I was hungry and now I won't even share a silly old rock. I'm ashamed of myself! Let's be friends again, OK? And you can use this rock anytime you please!

MYRTLE: Thanks a lot, Croaky. And I'm sorry that I got mad at you. Now, I think I'll take a swim. It's too pretty to sleep anyway.

CROAKY: Wait for me! I'm coming, too. *(Both exit together.)*

Twenty Dollar Bill

Characters: Two puppets — CROAKY, a frog; HAPPY JACK; live
  TEACHER.

HAPPY JACK: *(Entering)* **Hi, kids. Isn't it a beautiful day**
  (night)? **I'm sure glad the rain stopped. A little more
  rain and** *(Use your town's name)* **would only have been
  fit for frogs.**

CROAKY: *(Coming in)* **Did someone say something about
  frogs?**

HAPPY JACK: **Oh, hi, Croaky. I guess you like all the rain.**

CROAKY: **Not too well. A little rain is fine, but too much is
  too much! It washed all the lily pads out of my pond!
  Hope it didn't wash all the bugs away!**

HAPPY JACK: **You can have all those creepy, crawly old
  bugs. As for me, I like hamburgers, french fries and
  ketchup!**

CROAKY: **That sounds good, too, except for that ketchup
  stuff. Talking about bugs and hamburgers makes me
  hungry. I think I'll go catch a few bugs for supper. So
  long.** *(He exits.)*

HAPPY JACK: **Guess I'd better go, too.** *(Moves a couple of
  steps, then stops and looks down.)* **Say, what's that?** *(Stoops
  and comes up with a bill in his hand. Use toy paper money.)*
  Wow! A twenty dollar bill. To spend just on myself!
  (Kisses the bill noisily.) **You** *bee-utiful* **green stuff. Am I
  going to have a spree! Let's see — first I'll buy a huge
  juicy hamburger, a giant chocolate milkshake and —
  let me think. I'll finish it off with a banana split. Boy,
  oh boy!**

CROAKY: *(Entering)* **Say, Happy Jack, it looks like I'm
  out of luck for supper. The rain must have washed all
  the bugs away 'cause I can't find a one. I sure am hungry.**

HAPPY JACK: **That's too bad, Croaky. Look, I gotta go.
  I just found a twenty dollar bill and I'm gonna have a
  ball. And the first thing I'm gonna do is have a
  hamburger feast. Bye, now.** *(Turns to go.)*

TEACHER: *(Rising from a chair)* **Why don't you share your
  money with Croaky, Happy Jack?**

HAPPY JACK: **Huh? Huh! Nothin' doin'!** *I* **found it. Why**

should I share it with anyone?

CROAKY: I sure am hungry.

HAPPY JACK: Go find your own supper. This twenty dollar bill is mine.

TEACHER: The Bible says we are to share with the hungry and those in need.

HAPPY JACK: Does the Bible say that?

TEACHER: Yes, and it also says we are to love others as we love ourselves.

HAPPY JACK: Well — if the Bible says that . . . .

TEACHER: It also says we are to treat others as we want them to treat us.

HAPPY JACK: Well, that settles it! If Croaky had found a twenty dollar bill, I would sure have wanted him to share it with me. Come on, Croaky, let's go eat! *(Throws an arm about CROAKY and both exit together.)*

Real Love

Puppets: BETTY LOU, a girl frog puppet; CROAKY, a boy frog
puppet.
**ANNOUNCER: Let's go down to Marshy Pond and visit
with Croaky today. Are you ready?** *(CROAKY and BETTY
LOU appear at opposite sides of stage. CROAKY walks over
and kisses BETTY LOU loudly on the cheek.)*
BETTY LOU: *(Looking shocked)* **Stop that, Croaky! I don't
allow anyone to kiss me except my mother, father and
brother. What did you do that for, anyway?**
**CROAKY: Well — I saw a human down in the park kiss a
girl, and he told her he loved her. What is love, anyway?**
**BETTY LOU: Well, there's love for parents and love for
friends and . . . .**
**CROAKY: And love for bugs! I sure love bugs! To eat, I
mean.**
BETTY LOU: I don't think that's real love, Croaky.
**CROAKY: I guess not. But what is this kissing that
humans do?**
**BETTY LOU: Kissing is supposed to show love. You don't
just kiss anybody.**
CROAKY: That makes sense.
**BETTY LOU: I heard that preacher who teaches the kids
in the park every week talking about love.   He said
everyone should love God first and then neighbors as
we love ourselves.**
CROAKY: Who is my neighbor?
**BETTY LOU: The preacher said everyone is our neighbor.
So we should love everyone: our friends, parents,
cousins and . . . .**
CROAKY: My cousins are tadpoles.
**BETTY LOU: Be serious, Croaky! And stop interrupting
me! That preacher said we are even supposed to love
our enemies.**
**CROAKY: Love my enemies! I don't even *like* my
enemies! Right now, I don't even like Freddie and he
isn't my enemy. Do you know what that frog did? He
stole my bugs that I was saving for breakfast!**
BETTY LOU: Croaky, you need the God-kind of love.

CROAKY: What kind of love is that?

BETTY LOU: I heard that preacher say that God loved people so much that he gave his own son to die for their sins so they could go to heaven.

CROAKY: That was real love! If we had that kind of love, Marshy Pond would be a better place to live.

BETTY LOU: If you had *that* kind of love, you wouldn't be so mad at Freddie for stealing your bugs.

CROAKY: *(Thoughtfully)* Hmmm, I guess you're right.

BETTY LOU: And if you had *that* kind of love, you would forgive Freddie for stealing your bugs.

CROAKY: Yeah — you're right. OK, I forgive Freddie for stealing my bugs.

BETTY LOU: And Croaky, if you had *real* love for Freddie, you wouldn't mind sharing your bugs with him.

CROAKY: Sharing my bugs? I should say not!

BETTY LOU: But I thought you wanted Marshy Pond to be a better place to live.

CROAKY: Yeah, I really do. And I plan to do better. But if we are going to make Marshy Pond a better place to live, *you* have to change some things, too.

BETTY LOU: *(Shocked)* Like what?

CROAKY: How did you treat Myrtle the Turtle last week?

BETTY LOU: That dumb turtle? She's so slow — and besides she's different from us!

CROAKY: But she's still one of God's creations and as good as we are.

BETTY LOU: What makes you think that? We're better than turtles!

CROAKY: You said we are supposed to love our neighbors and Myrtle is our neighbor, even if she is a turtle. Remember the preacher said we should love our neighbors as ourselves.

BETTY LOU: You're right! If I want to make Marshy Pond a better place to live, I'll have to love Myrtle even if she is different from us frogs.

CROAKY: And Betty Lou, we'll both have to stop picking on Sammy the Snake just because he's smaller than we are.

BETTY LOU: Aw, do you really think we have to stop teasing

Sammy? *(Giggles)* He's so much fun to pick on. He "boo-hoos" so easily.

CROAKY: Teasing that little snake and making him cry isn't showing love and kindness. Think how he must feel!

BETTY LOU: I never thought about that! I sure wouldn't want anyone picking on me just because he was bigger than me! That preacher said one should treat everyone just like he wants to be treated. That's the Golden Rule.

CROAKY: I can see why they call it the Golden Rule. It makes sense! You know, I feel real good inside since I forgave Freddie and have decided to be kind to others!

BETTY LOU: You know, I do, too! You know what, Croaky? We have found out what *real* is! It's sharing, being kind to others and forgiving!

CROAKY: I'm going to try to love everybody. And especially you! *(Kisses BETTY LOU on the cheek.)*

BETTY LOU: *(Looking shocked)* Croaky!

Where's That Pin?

Puppets: GRANDMOTHER; LINDA, her granddaughter; JANET.

NARRATOR: **Linda is spending the summer with her grandmother.**

GRANDMOTHER: *(As she and LINDA enter)* **Good morning, Linda.**

LINDA: **Good morning, Grandma. I'm so glad you invited me to spend the summer with you. I'm having so much fun!**

GRANDMOTHER: **It's so good to have you, honey. Having a young person around again really livens up this old house.**

LINDA: *(Admiring brooch on GRANDMOTHER's dress. Pin a large dress pin to her dress before the scene opens.)* **What a beautiful pin. Are those real jewels?**

GRANDMOTHER: **My youngest son sent this brooch to me when he was in Germany. The jewels aren't real but I prize it highly because he gave it to me. He was killed in the war, you know.**

LINDA: **That was Uncle Herman, wasn't it? Mother told me he was killed while rescuing another soldier. He was a real hero.**

GRANDMOTHER: **Yes, I suppose he was a hero. He was a sweet boy and I still miss him. But he is in heaven with Jesus. Now — what would you like for breakfast?**

LINDA: **Oh, anything. Grandma, could I wear your pin sometime? I'd be awful careful with it.**

GRANDMOTHER: **No, child, I'm afraid you might lose it. It's very special to me. Now, come on and help me cook breakfast. I have some great plans for today.**

LINDA: **OK, Grandma.** *(Both exit and some lively music is played to denote a time lapse.)*

* * * * * *

(LINDA and JANET appear.)

JANET: **I'm glad your grandmother brought you over. What would you like to do?**

LINDA: Oh, just anything.

JANET: Do you like to play dolls?

LINDA: Sure — and it would be fun to play dress-up, too.

JANET: Say, that would be fun! There's a big trunk up in the attic that's just full of old clothes and hats.

LINDA: Why don't we pretend I'm my grandmother and you are your mother. We'll pretend I'm visiting you. I even have one of Grandma's pins to wear. *(Shows her GRANDMOTHER's special pin.)*

JANET: Oh, it's lovely! But should you be playing with that? That's your grandmother's special pin. I heard her tell my mother about it.

LINDA: I'll be very careful with it. And when I get home, I'll put it back in her jewel box and she'll never know. I just *had* to wear it! It's so beautiful!

JANET   Could I wear it too?

LINDA: Well — maybe just a little bit. But we must be very careful not to lose it.

VOICE: *(Calls)* Girls! Girls! I'm going down to the store. There's cookies and milk if you get hungry.

JANET: OK, Mother. *(Turns to LINDA.)* We're going to have a neat time! Let's go look at the dress-up clothes. *(Both exit. Music is played briefly.)*

NARRATOR: The girls have had a great time all day and it is now getting about time for Linda's grandmother to pick her up.

LINDA: *(As she and JANET appear)* I'm so glad I came to visit Grandma! I've had so much fun today. Will your mother let you come over to see me soon?

JANET: Oh, sure!

LINDA: Good! I'd better gather up my things. I hear Grandma's car. Oh, I almost forgot. You can give me Grandma's pin now.

JANET: I don't have it. You had it last, remember?

LINDA: I don't have it. I thought you did. Help me look for it, quick. *(Wails)* If I've lost Grandma's brooch, she'll never forgive me! *(Both search frantically.)*

LINDA: I've lost Grandma's beautiful pin. Bo-hoo-hoo. What will I do? Boo-hoo-hoo. *(GRANDMOTHER appears. JANET slips out.)*

GRANDMOTHER: Whatever is the matter, Linda?

LINDA: Oh, Grandma, I'm so ashamed! I took your special pin. I only meant to — to wear it a little and put it back. But we can't find it anywhere! Boo-hoo-hoo.

GRANDMOTHER: *(Sternly)* Linda, I told you not to wear my pin. Why did you do it?

LINDA: I — I know you told me I couldn't wear it. Boo-hoo-hoo. I guess because it was s-so pretty and I just wanted to so bad. Boo-hoo-hoo. Are you going to send me home, Grandma? Boo-hoo-hoo.

GRANDMOTHER: No, Linda, I'm not going to send you home but I'm very disappointed in you.

LINDA: I — I'm so sorry. Boo-hoo-hoo. Can you ever forgive me? Boo-hoo-hoo.

GRANDMOTHER: Of course I'll forgive you, dear, but I do expect you to do what I ask of you. It is very important that children learn obedience. If you don't, it will affect you all your life, and you will always be in trouble of some kind.

LINDA: *(Still sniffling)* What do you mean?

GRANDMOTHER: Even adults have to take orders — from the people they work for, from government officials and police officers. If you don't learn to obey your parents, teachers and other adults, it will be hard for you to take orders when you are grown. That's why some people can't keep a job, and aren't good workers. They don't like having to take orders from others and obey rules.

LINDA: You mean adults can't do what they want to do?

GRANDMOTHER: I'm afraid not. And the earlier we learn to obey those who are over us, the easier life will be. A good employee is one who can take orders and has a good spirit about it. Some become criminals and outlaws because they want to do their own thing regardless of who it hurts.

LINDA: I didn't realize how important it was to do what I'm asked to do. I'll try real hard from now on, I promise.

GRANDMOTHER: I'm glad, Linda. One good way to do that is to ask God to help you and to obey God in all things.

LINDA: I'll ask God to help me and also to forgive me for disobeying you. And I'm so sorry I lost your lovely pin, Grandma.

JANET: *(Coming on the stage from the end, speaking excitedly and holding up GRANDMOTHER's pin.)* I found it! I looked through all the clothes we tried on and found it pinned on a long evening gown.

LINDA: Thank you, Janet! I don't know why I didn't think of that. I guess I was too upset and feeling so guilty I wasn't thinking straight. But I've learned my lesson! I'll never take anything that doesn't belong to me again! And if I don't mind Grandma the rest of the summer, she has my permission to spank me!

GRANDMOTHER: Good! With that attitude I don't think I'll have to! *(She hugs LINDA and all three sink from sight.)*

Mean Ole Gert

Puppets: Two girls, GERTRUDE and SUZIE; school teacher, MISS JONES; PRINCIPAL, Mr. Jefferson.

NARRATOR: Gertrude is the school bully at the Christian School. She goes by the name of Gert, and today, as usual, Gert is trying to pick a fight. *(GERT and SUZIE appear.)*

GERT: *(Mockingly)* **Deah, deah, deah — Suzie has a new dress. Here, let me wipe off that dust.**

SUZIE: **You get away from me, Gert! Don't you dare put mud on my new dress!**

GERT: **You shouldn't have dared me. Now I'll have to rub this nice, squishy mud all over that pretty dress. Maybe I better put some in your hair too, to match your dress.**

SUZIE: *(Backing away and speaking shrilly)* **You put that mud on me and I'll tell the teacher on you!**

GERT: *(Mimicking)* **"I'll tell the teacher on you!"** Go ahead and tattle. I'm not afraid of that old teacher. *(Starts to put mud on SUZIE.)*

SUZIE: *(Shrieks)* **Miss Jones! Miss Jones! Help! Help!**

MISS JONES: *(Enters quickly.)* **Gert, put down that mud!**

GERT: **I will not and you can't make me!**

MISS JONES: **Gert, I'm your teacher and you must obey me or I'll take you to the principal's office.**

GERT: **Go ahead! I'm not afraid of you or that old principal!**

MISS JONES: **We'll see about that, young lady. You keep up this foolishness and you are likely to be expelled from school.**

GERT: **I don't care! I hate school anyway!**

MISS JONES: **Come along, Gert. It's a trip to the principal's office for you.** *(GERT sticks her nose in the air and all exit.)* *(Musical interlude)*

NARRATOR: **It's a few minutes later in the office of Mr. Jefferson, the school principal.** *(PRINCIPAL, then GERT appear.)*

PRINCIPAL: **You may sit over there, Gertrude.**

GERT: **I don't want to sit down. And don't call me Gertrude!**

PRINCIPAL: **Very well, stand if you like. Now, why were you putting mud on Suzie's new dress?**

GERT: She thinks she's so smart! Her and all her *fancy* clothes!

PRINCIPAL: You mean you are envious of Suzie's new dress?

GERT: Naw, I can have all the new clothes I want.

PRINCIPAL: Then why did you do such a mean thing?

GERT: She doesn't like me. Nobody likes me.

PRINCIPAL: The other kids would like you if you would be nice to them.

GERT: I don't care if they don't like me! I don't like them either. I don't like anybody!

PRINCIPAL: We all want people to like us, Gert.

GERT: *I* don't! You hate me and the teachers hate me and all the kids hate me! Even my mother hates me! But I don't care! I hate all of you, too!

PRINCIPAL: You don't like yourself, either, do you?

GERT: That's a crazy thing to say! Of course I like myself! I'm tough and mean and everybody is afraid of me!

PRINCIPAL: But you *really* don't like yourself, do you, Gert?

GERT: What do you mean?

PRINCIPAL: You would really like to be popular and do well in your classes and get along with the other kids, wouldn't you?

GERT: *(Tossing her head and speaking impudently)* I *could* be smart and popular if I wanted to. I can do anything I want to do!

PRINCIPAL: Then — why don't you try being good and kind, and study hard, Gert?

GERT: *(Angrily)* You sound just like my mother! She's always yelling at me and telling me I'm ugly, dumb and mean! She hates me!

PRINCIPAL: Surely she doesn't hate you. She's your mother.

GERT: She does hate me! Who *could* love a big, ole ugly, freckled-faced, red-headed dumbbell like me! Boo-hoo-hoo.

PRINCIPAL: I know someone who loves you.

GERT: Nobody loves me! Boo-hoo-hoo.

PRINCIPAL: God loves you, Gert.

GERT: God doesn't love me. He couldn't! I'm too mean!

PRINCIPAL: Gert, God does love you. His son, Jesus, died on the cross to set you free from being mean and hateful and unlovable.

GERT: I *can't* be different! I don't really want to be bad but I can't help it. Honest, I do try sometimes to be good — but I can't!

PRINCIPAL: God knows you can't be good, Gert.

GERT: *(Looking up in surprise)* He does?

PRINCIPAL: It's hard for any of us to be good without help. You just need Jesus in your heart to help you.

GERT: He can't help me! I'm real mean! Even Mother says so.

PRINCIPAL: Why don't you try him and see?

GERT: W-What do I have to do?

PRINCIPAL: Just tell God you are sorry you have been bad and then invite Jesus into your heart and life.

GERT: *(Hesitantly)* Well — OK. *(Bows head.)* Dear God, I don't know much about praying but Mr. Jefferson said you would help me if I asked. I'm a mean, dumb, hateful girl but I don't want to be. Please forgive me and please, Jesus, help me to be good and kind. Thank you, Amen. *(Soft Christian music is played as PRINCIPAL and GERT sink from sight.)*

NARRATOR: It is a week later. *(SUZIE and MISS JONES are walking to school together.)*

SUZIE: That was really a big rain we had last night.

MISS JONES: Yes, that was quite a storm. Say, that car is coming dreadfully fast! He'll splash us with mud if we don't get back! *(Both draw back.)*

SUZIE: Oh, no! That car splashed mud on my dress! Mother will be furious!

GERT: *(Appearing)* Here, Suzie, let me wipe off the mud with my handkerchief. *(She does so.)* Maybe it won't be too bad if you go right in and wash out that one bad spot.

SUZIE: *(Astonished and almost speechless.)* Th-thank you, Gert.

GERT: That's OK. I gotta run now. Mr. Holmes said he would help me with my math if I'd come in early. Bye now. *(Exits)*

SUZIE: I can't believe my eyes — and ears! Was that *really* Gert?

MISS JONES: That's what all the teachers have been saying for the past week. And yesterday Gert's mother stopped me on the street and wanted to know what we had done to her. She said Gert is just a different girl.

SUZIE: Do you suppose she got religion?

MISS JONES: I don't know, but I can say one thing: it's the greatest miracle I ever saw!

CHAPTER 8

New Testament Bible Lessons

- In the Pig Pen
- A Modern Good Samaritan
- Another Chance
- Bernard, the Third
- Meanness
- I'll Never Forgive You
- Mustard Seed
- Greedy Shep
- Freddie, the Brat
- Sowing Seed
- Lost

In the Pig Pen

Puppets: REUBEN, JOEL, FATHER, FARMER

NARRATOR: **Jesus once told a story about a rich man who had two sons. Perhaps this was a family Jesus knew. Jesus didn't tell the names of the individuals so we will just call the younger son Joel and the older one Reuben. It was very early in the morning and Reuben was ready to go to work in the fields.**

REUBEN: *(Comes on stage, looks back and calls.)* **Joel! Joel! Are you ready to go to work?**

JOEL: *(Comes out slowly and speaks crossly.)* **What do you want, Reuben?**

REUBEN: *(Sarcastically)* **It's time to go to work, you lazy sleepyhead. We have to plant the upper field in wheat today. Remember?**

JOEL: **Sure, I remember!** *(Mockingly)* **Time to go to work! Time to go to work! I'll tell you, I'm sick of working! That's all we ever do around here! Work! Work! Work! From daylight to sundown! Well, I'm fed up with it!**

REUBEN: **The Bible says a lazy man will come to poverty.**

JOEL: **You're just like Father! All you ever think about is work. But *I* want to have some fun. And I'm going to —— while I'm still young enough to enjoy it!**

REUBEN: **What are you going to do?**

JOEL: **I'm not sure yet, but I'll think of something. Then I'm having a talk with dear ole Dad!**

REUBEN: **You'll do anything to get out of work! Well, go ahead and cry on Father's shoulder! But *I've* got to go to work. That wheat won't plant itself, and I can see I'll not get any help out of you, baby brother!** *(Stalks out.)*

JOEL: *(Watches him go and then begins to walk back and forth slowly and thoughtfully. Suddenly he stops and speaks excitedly.)* **I've got it! I know what I will do!**

FATHER: *(Enters)* **What are you going to do, Joel?**

JOEL: **Oh, good morning, Father.**

FATHER: **I saw Reuben going to the fields. Why aren't you with him?**

JOEL: **Father, I don't want to work in the fields anymore. You have a lot of land and money. Someday all of it**

will be mine and Reuben's. So why can't I just have my share now. I want to go out and have fun while I'm still young enough to enjoy myself.

FATHER: They say, "A fool and his money are soon parted." If you take your share and spend it all foolishly, then what will you do?

JOEL: You let me worry about that, Father.

FATHER: (Sadly) Very well, Son, if that's the way you want it. I'll have your share ready as soon as you're ready to leave. (Exits)

JOEL: Yippee! I'll never have to work again! Let poor ole Reuben slave under the hot sun! His younger brother is too smart for that! Am I gonna have fun! World, here I come! (Exits)

(Play some soft music while JOEL's clothes are changed to rags.)

NARRATOR: So Joel took his share of his father's money, left his father's house and went into a far country. He began to spend his money on anything and anyone that pleased him. He drank and gambled and feasted and played. And never worked! And as long as his money lasted he had lots of friends.

But one morning he woke up to find that his money was all gone! He tried to borrow from friends but no one would loan or give him a penny. In fact, no one would even give him a crust of bread to eat, and the landlord threw him out in the street when he couldn't pay his rent!

He was in a bad way! Far from home, with nothing but the clothes on his back. He could find no work because there was a famine in the land. He became hungry — oh, so very hungry! He kept trying to find work because he knew he must work or starve.

JOEL: (Appears and knocks on door.) Please, sir, I need a job badly. I'll do anything.

VOICE: I don't need any help.

JOEL: Could you give me a piece of bread to eat, then. I'm very hungry.

VOICE: I don't feed bums!

JOEL: (Despairingly) What am I going to do? What am I

going to do? *(Pauses and looks around.)* **There's another door. I'll try there. I can't go much further, though. I'm so tired and weak from hunger.** *(Knocks on door.)* **Kind sir, do you have any work for me? I'll do anything.**

FARMER: *(Appears)* **I need someone to feed my hogs. You don't look too strong but I'll try you.**

JOEL: **Do you have anything besides feeding pigs?**

FARMER: **That's the only job I have. Take it or leave it!**

JOEL: *(Hastily)* **I'll take it. When do I start?**

FARMER: **Right now.**

JOEL: **Could you please give me a little food first? I am so hungry!**

FARMER: **Not a crust of bread do you get until you have put in a day's work! Now get to work before I change my mind!**

JOEL: *(Bowing humbly)* **Yes, sir.** *(Both exit.)*
        (Musical Interlude)

NARRATOR: **The job paid so little money that Joel could not even buy enough food to satisfy his hunger. He was so hungry sometimes that he felt like gobbling up the coarse beans that he fed the hogs. Finally one day he came to his senses.**

JOEL: *(Appearing)* **I've got to do something! I'm so hungry I could eat the pig's food and no one cares if I live or die! Even the servants in my father's house have plenty to eat and I'm dying of hunger. I'll go back to my father's house. He may not want me for a son now but maybe he will at least let me be a servant in his house.** *(Runs across stage and disappears.)*

FATHER: *(Appears at the other end of stage, shades his eyes and looks across stage as if looking down the road.)* **Joel has been gone for a long time. How my heart longs to see my boy. If only I knew he was all right.** *(Bows head.)* **Heavenly Father, please take care of Joel wherever he is.** *(Raises his head, shades his eyes again and looks into the distance.)* **Someone is coming down the road. Could that be Joel?** *(Takes a step forward.)* **He looks young but he is so thin and ragged.** *(Takes another step.)* **Could that be my boy? It looks a little like him.** *(Calls)* **Joel, is that you?**

JOEL: **Father!**

FATHER: *(Running and throwing his arms around JOEL and kissing him)* **My son, my son! You have come home.**

JOEL: **Father, I have sinned against God and against you. I am no longer worthy to be called your son. Just make me one of your servants and I'll be satisfied.**

FATHER: *(Shouting)* **Servants! Bring the best robe in the house and a gold ring and shoes. My son has come home! Kill the fat calf and prepare a feast. My son was dead and is now alive, he was lost and now is found! Let us be merry for my son has come home!**

A Modern Good Samaritan

(Based on the Good Samaritan parable in Luke 10:25-37)

Puppets: GRANDMOTHER; MARCY, the granddaughter; TOUGH, a male puppet; REV. MODERN; MRS. DO-GOODER; small, stuffed toy dog.

NARRATOR: Marcy was visiting her grandmother a while back when she learned what a Good Samaritan is. It all started one Sunday morning.

GRANDMOTHER: *(Calls)* Are you ready for Sunday school, Marcy?

MARCY: *(Entering)* I'm all ready. Sure wish you could come, too.

GRANDMOTHER: I'll miss being there. Maybe I'll feel better tonight. Listen real close and tell me about the sermon.

MARCY: OK, Grandma.

GRANDMOTHER: Did you study your Sunday school lesson?

MARCY: Sure did. It's about that good guy — the Samaritan — who took care of a poor guy that got beat up and robbed. A priest and a Levite came by first but they didn't want to get involved. They sound like a lotta people today, don't they? Say, who is a Samaritan, anyway?

GRANDMOTHER: Samaritans were part Jewish and part something else, sort of half-breeds. The Jews didn't like them. They considered themselves better than the Samaritans.

MARCY: You mean like most people feel about the folks who live across the tracks in those old shacks by the river?

GRANDMOTHER: *(Sadly)* I'm afraid so, Marcy.

MARCY: Grandma, you really can't blame people! Those guys across the tracks are always fighting and getting into trouble. They're dirty and use bad language and act awful tough. I guess they are tough! I'd sure hate to meet one by myself after dark!

GRANDMOTHER: Marcy, no doubt some of them fit that description, but I'm sure not *all* the people who live in that slum are like that. Some are just poor and can't help where they live.

MARCY: Well — maybe. Just the same, I'll bet there's not a one of them who would help someone on this side of the tracks if he was dying!

GRANDMOTHER: Marcy, I think the point of the Sunday school lesson is not who will help *us* but whom can *we* help. I believe God would consider them our neighbors and therefore we are to be concerned about them and their needs.

MARCY: I suppose. Well, I don't know any of them and I don't think I really want to. Now, I'd better run or I'll be late for Sunday school. *(Exits)*

NARRATOR: It is about ten blocks to the church Marcy attends. She is about halfway there.

MARCY: *(Appears, walks along, then stops suddenly.)* Say, what's that lying in the street? *(Takes a step and looks down.)* Oh, no! It's old Mrs. Johnson's dog; a car must have hit it. I sure hope he isn't dead. He's all she has and she loves him so much. *(Kneels)* He isn't dead but seems to be hurt real bad. I'll take him to Mrs. Johnson's house and then call the vet. Oh, no! Mrs. Johnson is visiting her sister across town for a few days. Her dog must have gotten lost and tried to come home. My, what can I do? He's too heavy to carry all the way home and besides, he needs a doctor right away. I can't leave him to get help. Sure wish someone would come by to help!

(REV. MODERN appears at other end of stage.)

MARCY: *(Continued. Looking around.)* I'm in luck! There's Rev. Modern, the pastor of that big church on the corner. He's a minister, so he'll help me. *(Calls)* Rev. Modern! Please help me get Mrs. Johnson's dog to a veterinarian. He's hurt bad.

REV. MODERN: *(Huffily, barely looking toward MARCY)* I have a large congregation of people who need my services more than a dog! Besides, I might stain my clothing.

MARCY: Please, Rev. Modern, this dog is like a child to old Mrs. Johnson. Please . . . *(REV. MODERN leaves without a backward glance.)* **Well! Some minister he is! He didn't even care! What can I do?** *(Pats dog.)* **Hold on there, little fellow! I'll get some help yet.** *(Looks up.)* **Thank goodness! There's Mrs. Do-Gooder from our church. She helps raise money for the missionaries so she'll surely help.** *(Calls)* **Mrs. Do-Gooder!**

MRS. DO-GOODER: Yes, *deah?*

MARCY: Please help me get Mrs. Johnson's dog to a doctor. He's hurt real bad.

MRS. DO-GOODER: *(Stopping to look and then looking away)* **Deah** me! The sight of blood makes me sick. Besides, I really must hurry on as I'm late already and I must make my mission report today.

MARCY: Please help me. Mrs. Johnson loves this dog so much and . . .

MRS. DO-GOODER: *(Interrupting)* If she loves him so much, why did she let him out on the street where he could get hit by a car. Let her take care of him. It's *her* fault. *(She walks away.)*

MARCY: *(Pleading, until MRS. DO-GOODER disappears)* Please, don't go away. Please help . . . . Talk about good Samaritans. I could sure use one about now! *(Looks down the street.)* As if I didn't have enough trouble! There's one of those toughs from across the tracks! Maybe if I sit real quiet, he won't notice me.

TOUCH: Hey there, kid, you got some kind of trouble? *(Comes closer.)* What's the matter with the pooch? The poor little dude. A car must have hit him. Right? *(MARCY nods yes.)* He looks in a bad way. I'll take him to the vet. There's one about a block from here. He'll fix him up in nothing flat.

MARCY: You — you mean you're gonna help me?

TOUGH: Sure! Why not? Help me lift the pooch up in my arms. Easy now. *(MARCY and TOUGH [holding dog] exit.)*

NARRATOR: It's about three hours later.
(GRANDMOTHER and MARCY appear.)

GRANDMOTHER: Well, Marcy, as late as you are, you must have had a good service. What was the sermon about?

MARCY: The sermon was "The Good Samaritan," but the minister didn't preach it. I had it acted out for me. I didn't even get to church.

GRANDMOTHER: You didn't? I don't understand.

MARCY: You remember we were talking about the Good Samaritan before I left, and about the toughs across the tracks?

GRANDMOTHER: Yes, I remember.

MARCY: Well, on the way to church, I found Mrs. Johnson's dog in the street. He was hurt bad; a car must have hit him. Anyway, I tried to get Rev. Modern to help me get him to a vet and he wouldn't. Then I tried to get Mrs. Do-Gooder to help but she wouldn't, either. And who do you suppose came to our rescue?

GRANDMOTHER: I have no idea.

MARCY: A tough-looking guy from across the tracks! Grandma, he was the nicest fellow, and he loves dogs. He even paid the veterinarian. I told him to charge it and we would see that it was paid. But when he heard the dog belonged to old Mrs. Johnson, he insisted on paying the bill. Said he didn't have a mother and it would make him feel good to pay the bill for an old lady. I've sure learned my lesson well today! I'll never judge a person again by the way he dresses or where he lives.

GRANDMOTHER: That young man sounds like a very nice "Good Samaritan." How is Mrs. Johnson's dog?

MARCY: He's gonna be fine.

GRANDMOTHER: Thank the Lord!

MARCY: And the Good Samaritan!

Another Chance
(Based on Barren Fig Tree parable in Luke 13:6-9)

Puppets: CROAKY, a frog; SHEP, a dog.

NARRATOR: **Let's wander down to Marshy Pond and look in on our frog friend, Croaky.**

(SHEP and CROAKY appear on stage.)

SHEP: **Hi there, ole buddy. What's the problem? You look upset.**

CROAKY: **I'm more than upset, Shep, I'm mad! Boiling mad!**

SHEP: **What happened?**

CROAKY: **It's that rascalacious cousin of mine, Rocky! He just drives me crazy!**

SHEP: **Your cousin Rocky? I thought he was a pretty nice fellow.**

CROAKY: **That's because you don't have to live in the same pond with him! I'm going to boot him right out of Marshy Pond today!**

SHEP: **What has he done?**

CROAKY: **What hasn't he done would be a shorter story! He pulls poor little Jimmy Snake's tail, tries to ride on top of Myrtle the Turtle's shell, muddies up the water so our fish neighbors can hardly breathe, and to top it all off, he tried to steal Betty Lou, my girl!**

SHEP: **If he stole your girl, she must not have cared for you much anyway.**

CROAKY: **I didn't say he stole my girl! She's as mad at him as everyone else is!**

SHEP: **Everyone else thinks he's a troublemaker, too?**

CROAKY: **I'll say! We had a pond meeting and everyone voted to throw him out of the pond! And since I'm his cousin they said I was the logical one to tell him that he isn't wanted here.**

SHEP: **Does Rocky know how everyone feels about him?**

CROAKY: **If he doesn't, he's an awful dumb frog!**

SHEP: *(Thoughtfully)* **Do you suppose he really doesn't know that what he does makes everyone mad?**

CROAKY: **Well, if he doesn't, he'll know it soon! As soon as I find him, I'm going to tell him he's not welcome here and I'll kick him out if he doesn't want to leave!**

SHEP: Have you talked to him about what he is doing?

CROAKY: Naw! He's a smart-alecky little twerp that thinks he knows everything. I'd be wasting my breath. He landed in our pond trying to tell everyone how to do everything. Thinks he knows more than anybody!

SHEP: My master, Mr. Brown, read his boys a story out of the Bible about a man who owned a fig tree that never did put on any figs.

CROAKY: What has the Bible and fig trees got to do with my smart aleck cousin?

SHEP: A lot, I think. The owner wanted to cut it down — get rid of it — just like you want to get rid of Rocky.

CROAKY: (Impatiently) OK, what happened to the fig tree?

SHEP: The man who took care of the trees asked the owner to give the tree another chance. "I'll dig around it and put fertilizer on it," he said, "and then if it still doesn't put on any figs, then out it goes."

CROAKY: Did it put on any figs the next year?

SHEP: I don't know. The Bible didn't say. But whatever happened, the tree did get a second chance. Would you be willing to give Rocky one?

CROAKY: I should say not! It wouldn't do any good anyway.

SHEP: How do you know if you don't try it? You could talk to Rocky. Tell him just what he is doing to make everyone mad at him. Then the choice would be his to straighten up or get out of Marshy Pond.

CROAKY: I don't think anyone else would go for it.

SHEP: Everyone deserves a second chance, don't you think?

CROAKY: (Grudgingly) Well, I suppose so. I'll see what I can do. But I warn you, if he doesn't straighten up his act, out he goes! (They shake hands or nod their heads to show it is a deal. Both exit.)

NARRATOR: It's been two days, so let's go down to Marshy Pond and see if Rocky got thrown out of Marshy Pond.

(SHEP appears, then CROAKY.)

SHEP: Hi, Croaky! Did your cousin Rocky get kicked out of Marshy Pond?

CROAKY: You won't believe this, Shep! I talked to Rocky and told him that everyone was disgusted with him for picking on everyone and acting like he knew everything.

SHEP: Did he get mad?

CROAKY: At first he did. Then suddenly he began to cry real loud. He said they had made him leave the last pond, too, and he didn't know why.

SHEP: So, he didn't know the things he did made people mad?

CROAKY: No, he just thought no one liked him. When he pestered everyone, he was just trying to get them to like him. And he thought everyone would think he was smart and like him if he acted like he knew a lot.

SHEP: What happened? Are you all going to let him stay in Marshy Pond?

CROAKY: Yep! Rocky told everyone he was sorry and we all voted to let him stay if he would act right.

SHEP: Is he acting right?

CROAKY: He's trying hard and everyone is trying to help him. Thanks, Shep, for talking me into giving him a second chance. I think I may even get to like that frog!
(Both exit.)

Bernard, the Third
(Based on parable of Talents in Matthew 25:14-30)

Puppets: SHEP, a dog; CROAKY, a frog.
(SHEP appears, sighing and slumped over despondently. CROAKY comes in.)

CROAKY: Hi there, Shep. What's wrong? You look terrible!

SHEP: Everything's wrong. I wish I had never been born!

CROAKY: Shep! That's an awful thing to say! You're usually so happy. What happened?

SHEP: Bernard, the Third, that's what!

CROAKY: Bernard, the Third? Who's he?

SHEP: We have some new neighbors and he's their dog.

CROAKY: You mean a new dog in the neighborhood has you looking this down and out? I thought maybe someone had died!

SHEP: Someone is dead! Me!

CROAKY: Come on, Shep, talk some sense! Of course you're not dead!

SHEP: I might as well be! And all because of Bernard, the Third!

CROAKY: Tell me about the illustrious Bernard, the Third.

SHEP: Illustrious? What does that word mean?

CROAKY: It means that a person is famous and highly distinguished, that his deeds are glorious and stand out.

SHEP: That's Bernard, the Third, all right. He can do *everything* and do it well. And he looks like a duke or a prince.

CROAKY: Why should you be upset over how Bernard looks or acts?

SHEP: Everyone is wild about him! You remember I told you about Goldie, that pretty collie down the street from me?

CROAKY: Sure, you're sweet on her.

SHEP: She never even sees me when Bernard, the Third is around. And he's around a lot because he likes Goldie.

CROAKY: So you're mad because he won your girl away from you?

SHEP: He's won everyone away from me. His owners brought him over to our house. They're friends of my humans, the

Browns. Anyway, they brought him over to show him off and now he's as welcome at our house as I am!

CROAKY: I think you're jealous, Shep!

SHEP: You'd be jealous, too! All I hear anymore is what Bernard, the Third can do, how he acts so gentlemanly, and what a marvelous blood line he has!

CROAKY: So, he's a dog with a pedigree?

SHEP: Oh, yes! *(Speaks in a high, mimicking voice.)* "Our Bernard, the Third has lots of champions in his background. And he's already won many ribbons. He's a real champion, you know!"

CROAKY: Is he a well-mannered chap?

SHEP: Around people he is — and around Goldie! And he can shake hands and bow and "speak" when they ask him to. He even puts his head up and warbles when they ask him to sing. People just go wild over him, petting him and giving him treats. It makes me sick!

CROAKY: Is he nice to you?

SHEP: No! He growls at me when no one is looking.

CROAKY: It sounds like he's not a nice fellow.

SHEP: You should see how handsome he looks! His owners take him to the Bow-Wow Beauty Shop every week to be groomed. He comes back all slicked up. They even put perfume on him!

CROAKY: Does he like that?

SHEP: Loves it! He goes around with his head high and just ignores mutts like me. But not Goldie. He struts in front of her house like a peacock. And she comes out and admires him and calls him Bernie. It makes me sick!

CROAKY: Do his owners take him to dog shows?

SHEP: All the time!

CROAKY: So Bernard, the Third is all you would like to be: handsome, pedigreed, admired, and groomed. Is that right?

SHEP: Well — I'm not sure I would like to be all the things he is, but I would like for people to like me like they do him. They forget me when he's around, even my humans and Goldie.

CROAKY: But you have lots of talents, too.

SHEP: I don't have any talents! Instead of being a full-blooded dog, I'm a mongrel. I have a shaggy coat that even one of those dog groomers wouldn't know what to do with. I don't know any tricks except to sit up and beg, and that's a dumb, undignified trick.

CROAKY: Don't you guard the Brown's house against burglars, and play with the two children and watch over them? Didn't you run a big dog away from David when it was about to bite him?

SHEP: Sure, but those aren't talents.

CROAKY: Yes, they are! There's a parable in the Bible I heard about once. A rich man gave three servants some talents to take care of for him. A talent can be gold or silver money, but it also means an ability to do something.

SHEP: What's that story got to do with me?

CROAKY: Let me finish the story and you'll see. The first servant invested his master's five talents and got five more, and the second did the same. But the third servant just hid the talent he received and didn't put it to use. His master was very angry with him.

SHEP: What does all this have to do with me?

CROAKY: Don't you see? You have been using the talents you have and you don't have to ever be ashamed. Our talents are not the same. Your talents are really much more valuable to your family than Bernard, the Third's.

SHEP: They are?

CROAKY: Sure they are! Besides, you wouldn't like to have to go to the beauty parlor every week and go to dog shows and sit still by the hour and have people poking you and judging you.

SHEP: You're right! I'd hate that! And you know, now that I think about it, I growled first at Bernard, the Third. So he might not be a bad guy, after all.

CROAKY: And here comes Goldie right now. She's calling you so she must still like you.

SHEP: Yeah! Thanks a lot, Croaky, for showing me I have talents to use! Bye! (SHEP runs Offstage, then CROAKY exits.)

Meanness
(Based on parable in Luke 12:42-48)

Puppets: SHEP, a dog; CROAKY, a frog.
(CROAKY and SHEP appear on opposites sides of stage.)

CROAKY: Shep! What's the matter with you? Goodness! You have your tail between your legs and act like someone has just beaten you.

SHEP: You're right. I've about had it!

CROAKY: Tell me about it. What's happened to you?

SHEP: The Browns — you know, the humans I live with — have company from out of town: Mr. Brown's sister, Grace, and her eight-year-old boy, Reggie.

CROAKY: Are they nice like your master?

SHEP: No! They're as mean as — as Diablo, that snake you told me about.

CROAKY: What have they done to you?

SHEP: Everything! That woman's name is Grace but she's sure misnamed. She ought to be called "meanness"! And her son is even worse!

CROAKY: You still haven't told me what they did to you.

SHEP: Well, first off, when they came down the sidewalk, I went running to greet them like I do all of the Brown's friends. And that woman kicked me right in the ribs and told me to get away, that she detested dogs.

CROAKY: Why didn't you stay away from her after that?

SHEP: I did — or tried to. But her son, Reggie, followed me everywhere. And every time he caught me he hit me, or pulled my tail. He even tried to ride me and he's a big fat kid!

CROAKY: Didn't the Brown family protect you from them?

SHEP: They tried to. Mr. Brown got pretty sharp with Reggie and told him to leave me alone. And Stevie and David, my master's sons, got real mad at Reggie for hurting me but he only laughed at them. They are only four and six years old and Reggie's eight.

CROAKY: Say, I'm sorry about all that, old friend.

SHEP: *(Despondently)* I hurt all over from the mauling Reggie's been giving me. I finally had enough of it and I growled at that big bully.

CROAKY: Did that do any good?

SHEP: Just got me into more trouble. Reggie's mother happened to hear me and she grabbed up her heavy purse and took after me, whacking me at every step and calling me bad names, like "dumb" and "stupid."

CROAKY: You poor dog! What did you do? Did you bite her?

SHEP: I'm not that dumb! Mr. Brown would never stand for me biting people, even if they are hateful and mean.

CROAKY: Then what did you do?

SHEP: I ran away! And I don't plan to go back until those meanies go home.

CROAKY: Atta boy! *(Thinks a minute.)* Maybe Mr. Brown will influence his sister and nephew to be more Christian while they are there and then they'll be kind instead of mean.

SHEP: That's the sad part of it. They both claim to be good Christians.

CROAKY: *(Shocked)* You're kidding!

SHEP: No, I'm not! That Grace woman talks all the time about the good things she does in her church. And I heard Reggie brag to Stevie that he got a prize for attending church for a year without missing once.

CROAKY: This is serious!

SHEP: Don't I know it!

CROAKY: You know what Grace and Reggie are like?

SHEP: What?

CROAKY: The story of the butler that the young preacher told about. He tells lots of stories on Saturdays in the park. I heard him tell the kids one story he called a parable. It came out of the Bible, he said.

SHEP: Yeah, what does a parable have to do with Grace and Reggie?

CROAKY: The preacher said that some people were like the butler that a rich man had. He left his whole house in the butler's care while he went away on a long trip. At first the butler was real kind to all the other servants. But after a while, when the master had been gone a long time, he began to treat them awful, knocking them around and all.

SHEP: *(Impatiently)* **But what has that got to do with Mr. Brown's sister and nephew?**

CROAKY: **Don't you see? The preacher said the parable was really talking about people who say they are Christians but they don't act like Christ. They're unkind to other people** . . . .

SHEP: **And to animals.**

CROAKY: **That's right! But God sees what they are doing and doesn't like it a bit. In fact, the preacher said that when the rich man came back he severely punished the butler and took his job away from him.**

SHEP: **And that means that God will severely punish those who are unkind and mistreat others.**

CROAKY: **Right! That's what the preacher said.**

VOICE: *(Calling from Offstage)* **Shep! Shep! Come here, boy!**

SHEP: **That's my master's voice. I'd better hide. I sure don't want to go back and be hit anymore!**

VOICE: *(Offstage)* **Shep, old boy. I know you're somewhere around here. Come on home, now. Stevie told me what Reggie and Grace have been doing to you so I sent them away. You don't have to be afraid. Come on, boy.**

SHEP: *(Excited)* **I can go home! Isn't Mr. Brown great! He's one of God's real Christians! If I were human, I'd want to be just like him! Bye, Croaky, I'm going home!** *(Waving, SHEP races away. CROAKY waves, watches him go, then exits.)*

I'll Never Forgive You!

(Based on parable of the unforgiving debtor in Matthew 18:21-35.)

Puppets: MARCY, a girl; SHEP, a dog.
(MARCY, facing away from the opposite end of stage, comes on stage, sputtering and shouting at someone who is not seen by audience. SHEP appears at same time and stares at MARCY.)

MARCY: *(Shouting)* **I'll never speak to you again! And don't you ever come over to my house again! I hate you! Do you hear me? I hate you! And I'll never forgive you! Never! Never! Never!** *(She turns away, sees SHEP watching her and breaks into tears.)*

SHEP: **Say, what was that all about?**

MARCY: **I — I'm sorry you saw me so m-mad, Shep, but I have a right to be mad. Do you know what that Beth did? And she claims to be my friend!**

SHEP: **No, but from how mad you are, it must have been something awful.**

MARCY: **It was! She broke my very best doll, Carole. The one I love better than all the others. And she did it on purpose! Boo-hoo-hoo.**

SHEP: **That is bad! Why did she do that?**

MARCY: **Because I accidentally broke her bracelet. She's an old meanie and I won't ever forgive her for breaking my doll! Never as long as I live!**

SHEP: **That's a long time to hold a grudge.**

MARCY: **I don't care! She deserves to be hated!**

SHEP: **I think I had better tell you a story that Mr. Brown, my master, told his two boys the other night.**

MARCY: **I don't want to hear a story! In fact, I'm going in the house and tell Mother what Beth did.**

SHEP: **I think you should hear this story. It's from the Bible.**

MARCY: *(Crossly)* **What do you know about stories out of the Bible?**

SHEP: **I know quite a few. Mr. Brown is a member of your church, and he tells his boys a story out of the Bible every night.**

MARCY: *(Ungraciously)* **Oh, all right, I'll listen to your story if you tell it fast. I can hardly wait to see what Mother thinks of Beth now! She thinks Beth is such an angel!**

SHEP: OK, here goes. Once upon a time there was a king
who gave a lot of money to his nobles to invest for him.
One day he called them all in and demanded them to
bring his money back so he could see how much they
had earned for him.

MARCY: Is that story really in the Bible? I don't remember
reading it.

SHEP: Sure it is! I'm just using my own words to tell it.

MARCY: OK, go ahead with the story.

SHEP: Well, one noble had lost all the king's money and
owed the king millions of dollars. He had invested it
poorly and didn't have any money to give the king.

MARCY: What did the king do?

SHEP: He ordered his servants to sell the noble as a slave,
and his wife and kids, too, and everything he owned
and pay the debt the noble owed.

MARCY: That was awful!

SHEP: Yeah, it would have been, but the noble fell on his
face before the king and begged the king to have
patience with him. He promised to some way raise the
money to pay him back. But do you know what the king did?

MARCY: Did he cut off the noble's head?

SHEP: Nope, the king felt sorry for the noble and told him
he forgave him, and to forget about the debt, too.

MARCY: So you are telling me that I am supposed to forgive
Beth for breaking my doll on purpose. No way! She
didn't even ask me to forgive her, but I wouldn't forgive
her if she did!

SHEP: That's not all the story.

MARCY: (Impatiently) OK, finish your story so I can go tell
Mother how mean Beth was. And I'm going to call up
all my other friends and tell them, too. Beth won't have
a friend left when I tell them what she did to me!

SHEP: There isn't much more to tell but here goes. The
noble went out the door of the king's palace and he
found a poor man who owed him a few dollars. He
demanded that the man pay him. In fact, he grabbed
the man by the throat and told him to pay up!

MARCY: That rascal! After the king had just forgiven him
for his big debt. What happened then?

SHEP: The poor man fell down at the noble's feet and begged him to have patience and he would pay the money. But the noble just grabbed the poor man and threw him into prison until he could pay his debt of a few dollars.

MARCY: That was horrible!

SHEP: Yes, but that still isn't all of the story. The king's servants heard the noble and they went and told the king.

MARCY: I imagine that noble was in deep trouble!

SHEP: You guessed it! The king had the noble brought to him. "You wicked man," he told the noble. "I forgave you of the big debt you owed me because I felt sorry for you, but you would not forgive the little debt that poor man owed you. So, you will go to prison until you pay all you owe me!"

MARCY: That served that mean old noble right!

SHEP: But that still isn't the end of the story Jesus told. He said that if a person will not forgive anyone who does him or her wrong, then God will not forgive that person. You must forgive to be forgiven.

MARCY: And you think I should forgive Beth! Well, I won't! *(Turns back on SHEP.)*

SHEP: I wasn't the one who said you should forgive her. The Bible did! To be forgiven by God, you must forgive!

MARCY: *(Stands still for a minute, then turns slowly back around and speaks slowly.)* I guess I forgot that I am a Christian. Even my best-loved doll is not worth displeasing Jesus. I'm dreadfully ashamed of how I acted, yelling at Beth and being so hateful. Maybe she thought I broke her bracelet on purpose. Anyway, I'm going to go call her and ask her to forgive me. Then I have to talk to Jesus and ask him to forgive me. Bye, Shep, and thanks! *(Exits)*

SHEP: *(Turns back toward audience.)* Those stories Mr. Brown tells out of the Bible sure pack a whallop! Even when a dog tells 'em! *(Exits)*

Mustard Seed
(Based on parable of Mustard Seed in Mark 4:30-32)

Puppets: MARCY, a girl; CROAKY, a frog.
(MARCY appears and begins to move along as if she is digging in ground and planting seed. Hums as she works.)

CROAKY: *(Enters)* **Hi, Marcy! Wha'cha doing?**

MARCY: **Hi, Croaky! I'm planting a garden. See, I've planted corn, peas, carrots, beets . . . .**

CROAKY: *(Interrupting)* **I can never understand why you humans are always planting and raising food. Why don't you just eat what God has provided, like I do?**

MARCY: **Because people don't like to eat grasshoppers and bugs like you do.**

CROAKY: **I keep forgetting that humans don't know that grasshoppers are some of the most delicious meat there is. Here, try one that I just caught. It's so fresh it's still warm.**

MARCY: *(Backs away)* **Uh-uh, no thanks. I don't want to offend you, Croaky, but grasshoppers are just not my idea of "delicious." I prefer vegetables. See, I've planted lettuce, green onions, mustard . . . .**

CROAKY: **I've heard of some of those other vegetables but I didn't know you grew mustard. Isn't that the yellow gooey stuff you smear on hamburgers and hot dogs?**

MARCY: *(Laughs)* **Not exactly. When I plant mustard seeds in my garden they come up and have crisp green leaves that are good in salads. The yellow gooey stuff you're talking about is made from the seeds. See, from these little seeds I'm planting.**

CROAKY: **Why not just eat the seeds instead of mashing 'em up into a yellow goop? Work, work, work! You humans go to so much work. Me, I just catch my bugs and eat 'em on the spot. No pots and pans or dishes to wash. And I sure wouldn't go to the work of digging up the ground and planting little ole seeds like that and hope they would come up and grow into food.**

MARCY: **I'll have you know that mustard seeds are very important seeds. The Bible even talks about them.**

CROAKY: **It does? What could it possibly say about little** ole mustard seeds?

MARCY: It says that the words of the Bible are like mustard seed.

CROAKY: You're kidding?

MARCY: Nope, I'm not. See how tiny they are? The Bible says that the words of God seem small like mustard seed but that when they are planted in the hearts of people, they grow into a big tree like a mustard seed does.

CROAKY: *(Scoffingly)* One of those little ole seeds couldn't grow into a tree!

MARCY: My pastor said that in Israel the land and climate are especially fitted to grow mustard, and that they grow so tall there that birds come and rest in their branches.

CROAKY: But what does the Bible mean when it says the Word of God grows into a tree?

MARCY: The Word of God — when it is preached and taught — changes wicked people into people of God. And all together the people become like a big tree that comforts and helps other people. In other words, the tiny seeds of God's word grow into a big tree, God's church.

CROAKY: You are lucky to be a human and get to be a part of God's church. It makes one want to be a human — but not when it comes to eating! Yuk! I can't stand that yellow mustard goop! Just give me bugs and grasshoppers any ole day and I'm happy. *(Both PUPPETS slowly sink from sight.)*

Greedy Shep
(Based on parable of the rich fool in Luke 12:16-21)

Puppets: SHEP, a dog; CROAKY, a frog.
(SHEP and CROAKY appear together.)

CROAKY: Hi, Shep. I haven't seen you for more than a week. Where have you been?

SHEP: Hi, Croaky. I've been busy, busy, busy.

CROAKY: Yeah? What have you been doing?

SHEP: Burying bones. And I'm just plumb worn out.

CROAKY: Burying bones? Whatever for?

SHEP: To eat, naturally!

CROAKY: What do you need to collect bones for? I thought the humans that you live with give you all the food you need.

SHEP: The Browns do take care of me. But I like to raid garbage cans for extra tidbits of food.

CROAKY: And that's where you found these bones you have been burying — in garbage cans?

SHEP: Not really. You see, I was going down the alley behind the big grocery store near our house to check their big garbage cans.

CROAKY: And you found a lot of bones?

SHEP: Not in the cans in back of the store. I was starting to turn one over when suddenly my trusty old nose caught the most delicious scent — of fresh meat.

CROAKY: Where was the meat?

SHEP: I stuck my nose in the air and just followed the scent. It came from a box behind a building just past the grocery store. I trotted over to the box and could hardly believe my eyes — or nose.

CROAKY: It was full of bones?

SHEP: Yep! It was plumb full of big bones just loaded with meat and fat. Not at all like the bones the Browns get for me. You know, the kind where the butcher all but scrapes the bones to get every bit of meat off?

CROAKY: Someone was sure wasteful to throw away bones with so much meat on them.

SHEP: Yeah. Mrs. Brown *buys* soup bones with less meat on them than those had.

CROAKY: Did you take some home for her to use?

SHEP: Naw. She has this funny notion that anything I carry in my mouth is dirty so she wouldn't have appreciated me bringing them to her.

CROAKY: So you buried them?

SHEP: Yep! I worked like crazy to get them all buried before any other dog saw them.

CROAKY: Wasn't that kinda greedy, not wanting to share?

SHEP: Why should I share? I found them. Let the other dogs find their own bones. Besides, they don't share with me.

CROAKY: Well, you have a whole box of bones buried so you shouldn't have to hunt for bones for a long time.

SHEP: I have six boxes full of good meaty bones buried!

CROAKY: (Shocked) Six boxes of bones?

SHEP: Yep! That was a new butcher shop and the other dogs in the neighborhood hadn't found out about it yet. And for six days there has been a box full of bones out back each day.

CROAKY: But where did you find places to bury all those bones?

SHEP: I dug holes in our backyard until Mr. Brown yelled at me to stop digging. Then I buried the bones all over the vacant lot near our house.

CROAKY: My, Shep, you are really clever! Imagine having all those bones to eat for months to come!

SHEP: (Proudly) Yep, I'm still worn out from all the work but it was worth it. It just takes brains and work to prepare for the future.

CROAKY: I'd like to see one of those super bones you were talking about.

SHEP: Sure, Croaky. I buried one right over here. Let me dig it up and show you. (Moves over and appears to be digging.) Here it is.

CROAKY: Yuk! What is that awful smell?

SHEP: It can't be!

CROAKY: Can't be what?

SHEP: Spoiled. It can't be, but it is! My lovely bone is spoiled! All that meat on it caused it to ruin!

CROAKY: (Turns his head away.) I'll say it's spoiled! Didn't you know meat would ruin if it isn't kept cold?

SHEP: No, I didn't. I never had but one bone at a time and
I always ate any meat there was before I buried it.

CROAKY: Poor Shep! All that work for nothing. You remind
me of the rich man in the Bible that I heard a preacher
in the park tell about one day.

SHEP: Did he bury bones, too?

CROAKY: Well — not exactly. The preacher said Jesus
told this story, or parable, about a rich man whose
lands produced so much food that he didn't have any
place to store it all.

SHEP: And he buried it?

CROAKY: No, but he was greedy just like you are. He
didn't share all that food with anyone. He tore down
all his big barns and built bigger ones to store it in.

SHEP: I don't think the rich man was so bad. He was just
planning for the future.

CROAKY: God called him a fool! And God said he would
not live to enjoy all that food because he was going to
die that night. And the food the rich man had laid up
in great storerooms would be eaten by other people.

SHEP: (Sadly) You're right, Croaky. I was greedy — just like
that rich man — and didn't think of anyone but myself.
If only I had shared those bones with the half-starved
dogs in our town. Now they won't do anybody any good.

CROAKY: Of course, you could still tell some of those
hungry dogs where the new butcher shop is so they can
get some bones, too.

SHEP: (Regretfully) The butcher shop no longer puts out
boxes of bones. The owner got smart. He trims them
real good now and sells them.

CROAKY: Well, at least you learned a lesson from this.

SHEP: Yep, I learned a lesson that I hope I never forget.
(Both exit.)

Freddie, the Brat
(Based on parable about rebellion in Luke 19:12-14)

Puppets: MARCY, a girl; SHEP, a dog.
   (MARCY and SHEP appear.)

MARCY: *(Angrily)* **I just had to get away from the house. That bratty boy just makes me sick!**

SHEP: What bratty boy?

MARCY: My Aunt Hattie's boy, that's who!

SHEP: Oh, the aunt who was going to visit you for a week?

MARCY: That's right. I looked forward to their coming because Aunt Hattie is really nice — but her Freddie is awful! Now, I can hardly wait for them to go home!

SHEP: What does Freddie do?

MARCY: What doesn't he do! At mealtimes if his mother tries to get him to eat his vegetables he throws them on the floor!

SHEP: Is he just a baby?

MARCY: Oh, he's a baby, all right, but not in age! He's eight years old and fat like a toad because he won't each much of anything except sweets.

SHEP: What does his mother do when he throws food on the floor?

MARCY: She says, *(In mimicking voice)* **"You shouldn't throw food on the floor, Freddie, dear." Can you believe that? Aunt Hattie is Daddy's sister and he told her she should turn Freddie over her knee and tan his britches for him.**

SHEP: Did she?

MARCY: She acted shocked when Daddy suggested spanking Freddie. "He's only expressing his likes and dislikes," she said.

SHEP: It sounds like your aunt is helping make a brat out of her son.

MARCY: I know, but no one can make her believe it. Mother is really worried about Freddie. She says he fights with his teachers and the kids at school and with everyone.

SHEP: I heard Mr. Brown, the human I live with, say that kids need to be taught respect for their parents and teachers and other adults or they never learn to get along with other people.

MARCY: That's what Daddy says, too. I'd be grounded till next Christmas if I talked to my parents like Freddie does!

SHEP: Mr. Brown said if kids didn't learn to respect their parents they wouldn't obey anyone, even God.

MARCY: I imagine he's right. My Sunday school teacher read us a parable last Sunday, from the Bible, about a nobleman who went into a far country to receive a kingdom for himself. But his citizens hated him and said they wouldn't have the nobleman rule over them.

SHEP: Was he a bad ruler?

MARCY: No, he was a super ruler. Our teacher said the ruler was Jesus. God, his father, had sent him down to earth to become our king. But many people didn't want Jesus to be their ruler.

SHEP: So they killed Jesus, the Son of God! I know, because Mr. Brown told his boys that story.

MARCY: That's right! But Jesus still has a kingdom — in the hearts of his people. We who want him to be the ruler of our lives can give our hearts to him and his spirit will come in and help us live good and happy lives.

SHEP: Maybe that's what Freddie needs: Jesus in his heart.

MARCY: You're right, Shep! Why didn't I think of that? He just follows me around bugging me, and I've just been trying to get away from him, instead of trying to help him. I think I could get him to go to Sunday school with me where he could hear about God.

SHEP: It sure wouldn't hurt to try it. In fact, why not get his mom to go, too? It sounds like they both need Jesus ruling in their hearts.

MARCY: I'll do it! I'm going home right now and invite them. And thanks a lot, Shep! For a dog, you're sure a smart cookie! *(Exits)*

SHEP: *(Watches her go, then speaks.)* **Just call me Deacon Shep!** *(Bows in direction MARCY disappeared, then exits.)*

Sowing Seed
(Based on parable of the Sower in Mark 4:3-20)

Puppets: CROAKY, a frog; SHEP, a dog.
(CROAKY and SHEP appear together.)

CROAKY: Shep, I heard that young preacher who teaches the kids on Saturday at the park tell a story that I didn't understand. Since you live at a Christian's house maybe you can explain it.

SHEP: I will if I can, Croaky. Tell me the story.

CROAKY: The preacher called the story a parable. You know what a parable is, I guess.

SHEP: Sure, a story out of the Bible.

CROAKY: That's right. Well, here's the parable: Once upon a time a man went out to plant a garden. He dug up his ground with a shovel . . . .

SHEP: Mr. Brown uses a roto-tiller to dig up his garden.

CROAKY: OK, maybe the man used a roto-tiller instead of a shovel. Anyway, after he plowed the ground, he began to plant the seed.

SHEP: Didn't he make any rows? Mr. Brown always makes rows in his garden.

CROAKY: *(In exasperation)* The preacher didn't say if he made rows or not. What difference does it make?

SHEP: It makes lots of difference! You don't just throw seed all over the ground — unless you are planting a lawn. And a lawn isn't a garden.

CROAKY: OK, OK! The gardener made rows and began to drop the seeds in the ground.

SHEP: What kind of seeds did he plant? Mr. Brown plants corn and peas and beans and radishes and . . . .

CROAKY: Would you please stop interrupting my story! I don't know what kind of seeds they were! The preacher didn't say!

SHEP: Why don't we just say they were corn then. I love fresh ears of corn, all drippy with melted butter. Mmmm, it's delicious.

CROAKY: OK, corn it is! Anyway, he dropped the seeds into the ground and some of it fell on a path . . . .

SHEP: He sure wasted his corn seed. He should have been

more careful.

CROAKY: Yeah, yeah, I guess so. But let me tell my story!

SHEP: I'm listening.

CROAKY: The birds came and ate up the corn that fell on hard ground.

SHEP: At least the birds in this story were smart.

CROAKY: *(In exasperation)* Do you want to hear this story or not?

SHEP: I told you I was listening.

CROAKY: Some of the seed fell on rocky ground where there wasn't much dirt.

SHEP: He ought to have known better than to put seeds in that kind of ground.

CROAKY: OK, smarty-britches. What happens to seed that falls on ground like that?

SHEP: If it's kept damp, the seed comes up real quick, but when the hot sun comes out, the plants just wither and die because the sun dries the ground as hard as clay.

CROAKY: Well, believe it or not, that's what the preacher said happened.

SHEP: Did the farmer plant any more seed?

CROAKY: Yep, and it fell among some thorns and soon the thorns choked the young plants so they didn't put on any grain.

SHEP: It sounds to me like that dumb gardener didn't dig up his ground well enough. I don't think he used a roto-tiller, after all.

CROAKY: Maybe he didn't, but I'll have you know that the rest of his seed fell into good, well-plowed ground and he had a super harvest from them.

SHEP: That's a relief. I was beginning to think he had wasted all his seed.

CROAKY: Well, he didn't. Now, Shep, what do you think is the meaning of the story?

SHEP: I guess everybody in his family had all the sweet, crunchy ears of corn they could eat. Wish I had one right now.

CROAKY: Shep! There was a lesson in the parable! The preacher said so.

SHEP: *(Chuckling)* I know there was. I was just kidding you.

I heard Mr. Brown tell that story to his two little boys, Stevie and David, and he explained it to them.

CROAKY: Well, tell me what the lesson was.

SHEP: It's really very simple: The seed is the Word of God — from the Bible. The farmer was the teacher or preacher who sows it or gives it out. The ground is the hearts of human beings.

CROAKY: Wow, you do know what it's all about!

SHEP: Yep, I've got a good rememberer. Well, the first seeds fell in hearts that didn't hang onto it and the devil came and stole it from their hearts.

CROAKY: Then it wasn't the fault of the gardener but was the fault of the ground?

SHEP: Right! The second batch of corn fell in shallow hearts that took it right in, but when the bad times came, they let the word die in their hearts.

CROAKY: They were as dumb as the first people.

SHEP: You can say that again! The third batch of seed fell in hearts that still had the roots of the world in them so the cares of the world, the desires for riches and other things choked them until the Word of God couldn't grow strong in their hearts.

CROAKY: I know what the last seed did. It fell into hearts that really wanted the Word of God in them so they became real Christians.

SHEP: That's right! And that's the only kind of Christians who are sincere. If I was a human, I'd be a real Christian.

CROAKY: Me, too! *(Both exit.)*

Lost!
(Based on parable of lost sheep in Matthew 18:12-13)

Puppets: SHEP, a dog; CROAKY, a frog.

SHEP: *(Appears on left side of stage.)* **I can't believe that I could be so stupid! My master warned me not to get lost, but I never thought it could happen to me!**

CROAKY: *(Comes in on right side of stage.)* **Shep! What are you doing up here in the mountains so far from home?**

SHEP: **Croaky, you're a sight for sore eyes, ole buddy! I'm lost, that's what!**

CROAKY: **Lost? How did you get up here in the mountains, anyway? Did you chase a rabbit clear up here?**

SHEP: *(Disgustedly)* **You're partly right. I came on a picnic with my humans — you know, the Brown family. A rabbit jumped up and I couldn't resist chasing him. When he finally ran in a hole, I tried to find my way back to the picnic grounds and couldn't.**

CROAKY: **You're always bragging about your good hunting nose. Couldn't you even follow your own trail back to your humans?**

SHEP: *(Defensively)* **I do have a good nose! I can trail with the best! But it suddenly started to rain and washed away the scent of my back trail.**

CROAKY: **You had better find your way back home quick because I can feel a snowstorm in my bones.**

SHEP: **Don't you think I know that! And if you're so smart, what are you doing up here in the mountains away from your warm pond?**

CROAKY: *(Condescendingly)* ***I* have everything under control, old friend. I came up here in the mountains to visit my cousin. I was on my way back when it started to rain and turn cold. I . . . .**

SHEP: *(Interrupts excitedly.)* **Do you know the way home? I'll just follow you home!**

CROAKY: **Sorry, old pal, but I'm a cold-blooded critter, so I can't go home right now. I'd get stiff from the cold and freeze to death.**

SHEP: *(Sarcastically)* **I thought you said you had everything under control!**

CROAKY: Oh, I do — I do, I assure you. *(Points or nods his head behind him.)* See that little pond over there? I plan to dig down in the mud at the bottom of it and hibernate until spring.

SHEP: Hibernate? What's that?

CROAKY: Bears and frogs and other wild critters go into a deep sleep during winter. We don't have to eat or drink; just live off our fat until spring comes again. Why don't you try it?

SHEP: You know dogs can't hibernate! If I didn't freeze to death, I'd starve to death! Besides, I couldn't breathe buried in the mud at the bottom of a pond!

CROAKY: I'm really sorry about that. What are you going to do?

SHEP: *(Despondently)* Try to find my way home, I guess.

CROAKY: Maybe the Browns didn't go home without you.

SHEP: Yes, they did. I finally found the picnic grounds but they were gone. Afraid of the coming snowstorm, I guess.

CROAKY: But I thought you said they loved you. If they loved you, why did they go off and leave you?

SHEP: *(Defensively)* They do love me! But Mr. Brown would have to see to the safety of his wife and two kids first. After all, I'm just a mutt they got from the dog pound a couple of years ago. *(Voice begins to quiver.)* I'm not worth anything and they can always get another dog at the pound lots prettier than me. Boo-hoo-hoo.

CROAKY: *(Pats his friend's arm.)* That doesn't sound like real love to me! I'd never do that to someone I loved! I'd sure help you if there was some way I could.

SHEP: I know you would, Croaky. But I think you had better go now and dig yourself a bed in the bottom of that pond. That gust of wind just now was bitter cold. Brrr.

CROAKY: *(With chattering teeth)* You're right, old friend, I'd better dig in before I get too cold to dig. Bye now, and I hope you get home some way and that I see you when winter is over. *(Waves and moves off to the right.)*

SHEP: *(Shivering as he walks back and forth)* That wind is sure getting cold. And now the snow is beginning to come down. What am I going to do? I mustn't panic. Gotta use the ole noggin. Let me think. Which way is home? *(Wails)* **I don't know! If only I had watched how we came up here.**

(Suddenly slumps over.) **If only I was a fancy poodle or some kind of expensive pedigreed dog, then maybe Mr. Brown would come back and try to find me. Boo-hoo-hoo. This is the only time I ever wished I was really *worth* something. I'm so lonesome I could howl. In fact, I think I will.** *(Howls.)*

VOICE: *(Offstage, calling)* **Shep? Is that you?**

SHEP: **That's my master's voice! But it can't be. He wouldn't risk his life in a storm to come back for a useless mutt like me! Would he?**

VOICE: *(Offstage)* **Shep! Come over here, boy. I've been searching everywhere for you!**

SHEP: **It is my master! He loves me! He came back! Here I am, Mr. Brown! I'm coming! I'm coming!** *(Rushes Offstage to right.)*

(Teacher should explain that Jesus loves us all and is looking for us if we are not safe in his fold, just as Mr. Brown came looking for Shep, and the shepherd came looking for his lost sheep; he rejoices when he finds each lost child.)

CHAPTER 9

Special Days Scripts

- A Valentine Lesson
- An Easter Story
- Trick or Treat
- A Witchie Story
- A Gift for Mother
- No Cornbread Dressing

Valentine Lesson

Puppets: RALPHIE, church mouse; CROAKY, frog; two other
puppets.

RALPHIE: *(Appears and speaks to himself.)* **There's a valentine
party at church tonight and I think I know how to
wangle an invitation. After all, I live in the church and
I should be invited! I get kinda tired just eating the
leftovers from church suppers and parties. Here comes
Marcy. I'll get her to help me with my plan.** *(Calls)* **Marcy!**

MARCY: *(Entering)* **Hi, Ralphie.**

RALPHIE: **Hi there. Would you give this valentine to the
pastor for me?**

MARCY: **Sure, Ralphie. And that is very nice of you to give
the pastor a valentine.** *(She accepts valentine and moves
out the other end of the stage.)*

RALPHIE: *(Chuckles and speaks in stage whisper.)* **I'm a smart
cookie, I am! I had to spend a whole fifty cents for that
valentine card but the pastor will feel obligated to invite
me to the church valentine party now.**

CROAKY: *(Comes onto stage near RALPHIE.)* **I heard that,
Ralphie! Aren't you ashamed to use a valentine for such
a selfish purpose?**

RALPHIE: **Well, I — I . . . .**

CROAKY: **A valentine is supposed to show that you love
someone. L-o-v-e, love! That's what valentines are all
about. Love, Ralphie, Love! What does your valentine
mean? That you love yourself, that's what!**

RALPHIE: **How do you know so much about it? You live
down in that muddy old pond all the time. You probably
wouldn't even want to go to a party. And besides, what
do you know about love? I live in the church building
and hear sermons on love all the time.**

CROAKY: **They sure didn't do you any good! You act like
some people I've heard about. Go to church all the
time and don't have the foggiest idea about what love
means. They cheat and lie and gossip about other Christians and go to church on Sunday and sing, "Oh, How
I Love Jesus."**

RALPHIE: **You know *I* would never cheat and lie and**

gossip . . . .

CROAKY: No, but yet you send a valentine to the pastor and act like you love him, when really all you want is an invitation to a party! That's being a hypocrite! Disgusting, that's what it is! *(Turns away and exits abruptly.)*

RALPHIE: *(In a mournful voice)* Now Croaky doesn't like me. In fact, I don't like me, either. He's right, I shouldn't have used a valentine for such a selfish purpose. *(Looks down the street.)* Uh-oh! This doesn't seem like my day! There's Shep and I imagine he's still mad at me for that dumb practical joke I played on him. Maybe I can get away before he sees me. Naw — he already sees me and is coming on the run. I guess I'll get a black eye out of this!

SHEP: *(Coming up all out of breath)* Hi, old pal. I have a valentine for you.

RALPHIE: For me? *(Suspiciously)* What's wrong with it?

SHEP: Not a thing. It's one of my nicest ones because you're my friend.

RALPHIE: You mean you still want to be friends after I played that mean trick on you last week?

SHEP: Well, I'll admit I was really mad at first; but then I thought of all the nice things you have done. I decided one bad joke shouldn't ruin a good friendship like ours. This valentine is to tell you I still want to be friends.

RALPHIE: Say, that's great! And I'm sorry about that practical joke. I have a valentine card for you, too, but I was afraid to go see you. It sure feels good to be friends again.

SHEP: *(Handing card to RALPHIE. If puppets have no hands or hands can't be manipulated, have them use their mouths to give and accept cards. RALPHIE could lay card down before he speaks.)* It sure does! Now I'd better go. I've got to deliver some more valentines. So long!

RALPHIE: Bye, and I'll get your card over to you later today. *(SHEP exits.)* So that was what Croaky meant when he said a valentine card was supposed to show love. That's sure what Shep meant to show me. And my valentine to the pastor didn't really mean anything.

But maybe I can change that! I want to show love, too. I see Marcy down the street. *(Calls)* **Marcy!**

MARCY: *(Enters from other end of stage.)* **Yes, Ralphie?**

RALPHIE: Have you delivered my valentine to the pastor yet?

MARCY: Not yet, why?

RALPHIE: When you deliver it, just tell him it's from a friend. Don't tell him it's from me.

MARCY: OK. *(Turns to leave and then turns back.)* By the way, Ralphie, I want to invite you to the church valentine party.

RALPHIE: Because I gave the pastor a valentine?

MARCY: No, because you're my friend. I've been meaning to ask you all week.

RALPHIE: Then I'll be happy to come.

An Easter Story

Puppets: CROAKY, a frog; SHEP, a dog.

SHEP: Hi, Croaky.

CROAKY: Hi, Shep. What brings you down to the park this afternoon?

SHEP: The kids from that church over on the corner are having an Easter egg hunt here today. So I thought I'd just mosey on over. If they accidentally leave any eggs, I'll use my trusty ole nose to find 'em. For my own use, of course.

CROAKY: Eggs don't sound very good to me, but everyone to his own poison, they say. I prefer bugs, myself. Say, how are Easter eggs different from just plain eggs?

SHEP: Well, Easter eggs can be either candy, or boiled chicken eggs colored up real pretty. Either one is delicious. Yum-yum. `

CROAKY: What do eggs have to do with Easter, anyway?

SHEP: *(Thoughtfully)* Well — let me see. I remember the people I live with talking about Easter and all. Hmmm. Oh, yes, now I remember. Mr. Brown said that Easter morning was when Jesus, God's son, was resurrected from the grave.

CROAKY: Resurrected? What's that?

SHEP: It's someone coming back to life after they've been dead.

CROAKY: You mean Jesus, God's son, died?!

SHEP: Yep! He didn't have to die, but he let some mean ole people kill him on a cross.

CROAKY: What did he do that for?

SHEP: Mr. Brown said all people have sinned. That's doing bad things. Anyway, he said that the sins must be paid for. Jesus loved people so much that he gave his life on the cross to pay for their sins.

CROAKY: He must have really loved people to give his life for them.

SHEP: He did. Mr. Brown said that Jesus never sinned at all himself, but that he went to the cross with the sins of the world on his back.

CROAKY: Say, that was great!

SHEP: Yeah. And the only thing people have to do to have
         their sins forgiven is to believe that Jesus died for them,
         ask forgiveness for their sins and live for God. Then
         they go to heaven when they die.
CROAKY: You said Jesus died and came alive again?
SHEP: Sure, and they buried him in a rock tomb. Three
         days later an angel came down and rolled away the big
         rock over the door and Jesus came out alive.
CROAKY: Wow! That's something! But you never did say
         what eggs have to do with Easter.
SHEP: Well — I don't know, unless it's because a little
         chicken lives inside an egg, like Jesus in the tomb, and
         when the time comes, the baby chick breaks open the
         shell and comes out alive, just like Jesus did from the
         tomb.
CROAKY: That makes sense.
SHEP: Mr. Brown says that people who accept Jesus as
         their savior will be resurrected, too, just like Jesus
         came out of the grave alive.
CROAKY: Aw, that's hard to believe.
SHEP: Not really. Did you ever see a caterpillar?
CROAKY: Sure. I eat them whenever I find one!
SHEP: You and your bugs and worms! Well, anyway, if you
         let a caterpillar alone — and don't eat him — after a
         while he will build a tight little case around himself,
         like a tomb, and you can't see him.
CROAKY: Sure, I know that, but what has that to do with
         people coming out alive again?
SHEP: Stop interrupting me and I'll tell you. After a while
         that ole caterpillar breaks open his tomb and comes
         out. But he isn't an ole worm anymore. He has a new
         body. He is a beautiful butterfly or moth, like we see
         flying around.
CROAKY: Yeah, I eat them, too, when I can catch 'em.
         But what has that to do with people?
SHEP: When they die they're put in a grave. And then in
         the resurrection, they come out alive — but with a
         beautiful new body!
CROAKY: Say, that's great!
SHEP: *(Turning head to look)* I see the kids coming for the

Easter egg hunt, so I'm gonna mosey on over there. Maybe if I do my sit-up-and-beg act, one of the kids will slip me an egg. Do you want to come with me?

CROAKY: Naw, but if you find any ole caterpillars or bugs out there, save 'em for me.

SHEP: Aw, you and your yukky bugs and worms! I'm gonna go hunt Easter eggs!

CROAKY: Heh-heh-heh.

Trick or Treat

Puppets: CROAKY, a frog; SHEP, a dog.

SHEP: I wonder where ole Croaky is. I've been all around Marshy Pond and I can't find him anywhere. *(CROAKY comes up panting.)* Oh, there you are! Where have you been?

CROAKY: *(Panting)* I've been downtown and am I ever glad to get home to my quiet pond!

SHEP: What's going on over there?

CROAKY: Witches and goblins and every kind of weird creature you can imagine, that's what!

SHEP: Witches and goblins? You mean real ones?

CROAKY: Naw! Not real ones! It's Halloween and the kids are dressed up in costumes. They're going from house to house trick or treating.

SHEP: Trick or treating?

CROAKY: Yeah! They yell "trick or treat" and people give them treats of candy and gum and apples.

SHEP: Say, that's fantastic! I'm gonna go, too. I love candy and gum, don't you?

CROAKY: Not really. I'll stick to my grasshoppers and bugs.

SHEP: Yuk! I'm gonna go get some of that candy!

CROAKY: Hey, not so fast! It's dangerous to trick or treat unless you know the humans you get the treats from.

SHEP: Dangerous? What do you mean?

CROAKY: Some humans are as weird as Halloween costumes. They like to put poison and razor blades and pins in the treats they give the kids.

SHEP: How awful!

CROAKY: Yeah. The rescue unit came screaming into town about the time I got there. A little kid was doubled up with pain and they were afraid he had been poisoned from candy someone gave him.

SHEP: Poor little guy! How could anyone do such a thing?

CROAKY: That's what I say! But you know, I saw some other bad things tonight. Some big boys — they looked like teen-agers — were standing around in the shadows, dressed up in costumes so nobody would know them. When little kids would come by with sacks full of goodies, they would jump out and grab their sacks and run away laughing. The poor little kids would cry like their hearts were broken.

SHEP: Mean, mean! They should be ashamed!

CROAKY: Some big guys were using soap on people's windows and some were even throwing raw eggs at houses. And I saw someone throw a balloon filled with water out a window on the trick or treaters. One poor little girl had on a red and green crepe paper dress and it was all soaked.

SHEP: There doesn't seem to be much good about Halloween, does there? But I did hear that *(Use your church name)* was having a good kind of Halloween party!

CROAKY: A good kind? That I've got to see.

SHEP: Come on over with me and I'll show you. There's not going to be any weird costumes like monsters or vampires. They're having a treasure hunt, some games and lots of goodies to eat that don't have any poison or pins in them. And there will probably be a story.

CROAKY: Say! That sounds like fun! Do you suppose they'll have some real treats — like bugs and grasshoppers — and maybe some of those dee-licious green beetles and . . . .

SHEP: *(Interrupting)* Please, Croaky, spare me. You're making me sick! I don't think they'll have any bugs but you can bring your own. Come on, let's go!

CROAKY: OK, but wait till I get my jar of bugs.

A Witchie Story

Puppets: Two puppets of any kind; SAUL, with crown on head; CAPTAIN; WITCH.

(HAPPY JACK and TEDDY come on stage from opposite ends.)

HAPPY JACK: Hi there, Teddy.

TEDDY: Hi, Happy Jack. Let's pretend to be humans and go trick or treating tonight.

HAPPY JACK: *(Doubtfully)* I don't know. I never did go before. What do we do?

TEDDY: I never did either, but humans dress up like witches, goblins or clowns and go up to a door and yell "trick or treat."

HAPPY JACK: Then what happens?

TEDDY: The people in the house give out treats of candy and gum and other good stuff.

HAPPY JACK: Say, that sounds like fun. What will we dress up like?

TEDDY: *(Chuckles)* Nothing. We aren't people anyway, so we'll go just like we are and people will think we're dressed up.

HAPPY JACK: Yeah! That's right! They'll never know we aren't kids in costumes. Although, now that I think of it, it might be fun to dress up.

TEDDY: OK. *(Turns as if to go. WITCH bobs up, skips along, then drops off the stage.)*

HAPPY JACK: Was that a people?

TEDDY: Yep! That was a kid dressed up like a witch.

HAPPY JACK: Why do they dress up like witches? Is there such a thing as a witch?

TEDDY: Some folks claim to be witches. I heard a preacher once tell a story from the Bible. It had a witch in it.

HAPPY JACK: It did? Tell me about it; I want to know about witches.

TEDDY: Well, it happened a long time ago. A man named Saul was the king of Israel. *(TEDDY and HAPPY JACK sink from sight and KING SAUL rises. TEDDY continues his story.)* King Saul was tall and handsome, but he was a weak king and stubborn, too, and he just wouldn't obey God, even though God had chosen him to be king. So

God finally got tired of his disobedience and turned away from him.

HAPPY JACK: Then what happened to him? And what about the witch?

TEDDY: I'm coming to that. Don't rush me! Well, a big army came to fight Israel and Saul was afraid because he knew he wasn't serving God and God wasn't with him anymore.

CAPTAIN: *(Appears and bows to KING SAUL.)* **King Saul, the enemy is not far away. What shall we do? Shall we prepare to fight?**

SAUL: Did you call in some prophets to inquire of God what we should do, as I instructed you?

CAPTAIN: Yes, sir. But I couldn't find any. Remember, you said to kill all of God's prophets that we could find.

SAUL: Yes — yes, I remember. I could sure use one of them now. I wish the prophet Samuel was here. He could tell us what we should do. He would have to die when we need him so badly!

CAPTAIN: That is true, sir. Samuel was the greatest of God's prophets.

SAUL: *(Excitedly)* I know what we can do! Find me a woman with a familiar spirit — a witch.

CAPTAIN: A witch? But, King Saul, you had all the witches and sorcerers killed, too. Remember?

SAUL: *(Impatiently)* I know! But you can't tell me you found them *all!* Surely you know where one is.

CAPTAIN: Well — yes. They say that a witch lives at Endor. But what do you want with her?

SAUL: I'll have her talk to Samuel's spirit and ask what we should do about the battle. *(Both exit.)*

TEDDY'S VOICE: King Saul and two soldiers disguised themselves and went at night to the witch at Endor. She was something like a modern medium or fortune teller. *(WITCH appears. A knock is heard. WITCH pretends to open door at end of stage, admitting KING SAUL without his crown.)*

SAUL: Old woman, I want you to bring up a spirit for me.

WITCH: I can't do that. King Saul will find out and have me killed.

SAUL: I promise you won't be hurt. Now bring me up the spirit of Samuel.

WITCH: Very well. *(She acts like she is going into a trance, then exclaims)* You are King Saul!

SAUL: Yes, I am, but don't worry. I won't harm you. Now tell me what you see.

WITCH: I see an old man, covered with a mantle.

SAUL: It must be Samuel. *(Looks down.)* Samuel, please tell me what we should do. If we fight with the enemy, will we win?

VOICE OF SAMUEL: *(Distinct, but slow)* You will not win. You and your two sons will be killed in the battle tomorrow. *(SAUL groans in anguish and falls to the ground in fear. WITCH and SAUL sink and disappear. HAPPY JACK and TEDDY enter.)*

HAPPY JACK: Then what happened?

TEDDY: King Saul and his two sons were killed the next day in the battle because Saul wouldn't serve God and because he went to a witch.

HAPPY JACK: Then God doesn't like people to go to mediums and try to talk to the spirits of the dead?

TEDDY: That's right! The preacher said witches and fortune tellers are fakes, but if they were real, they'd get their power from the devil. He said the Bible says people are not supposed to go to fortune tellers, mediums or use horoscopes or those ouiji boards. People should leave the future in God's hands.

HAPPY JACK: That makes sense! Thanks for the story. Now — let's go trick or treating, but I don't think I want to dress up like a witch.

A Gift for Mother

Puppets: GRANDMOTHER; MARCY, her granddaughter.
(GRANDMOTHER is in living room. A knock is heard. She answers the door.)

GRANDMOTHER: Hello, Marcy! This is a pleasant surprise. Come on in.

MARCY: *(Entering)* Hi, Grandma. I need your help to think up a gift for Mother. Mother's Day is the day after tomorrow and I just can't think of what to get her.

GRANDMOTHER: That shouldn't be hard. I'm sure she would be pleased with anything you get her.

MARCY: I know, Grandma. She isn't hard to please, but I would like to get her something very special this time. I want to show her that I *really* do appreciate all the things she does for us.

GRANDMOTHER: It sounds like my little granddaughter is growing up.

MARCY: Maybe I am. I got to thinking about how she always has our clothes washed, fixes us good meals and if we have a problem, she's always ready to listen. In other words, she's always there when we need her. And most of the time we don't even say thank you.

GRANDMOTHER: You do have a good mother, Marcy, and it does my heart good to hear you say you appreciate her.

MARCY: I do thank the Lord for Mother. But back to the gift. What am I going to get her that is special?

GRANDMOTHER: You could give her the gift she gave me when she was about your age.

MARCY: What gift was that?

GRANDMOTHER: She gave me a card and inside the pretty card was a list of the things she was giving me.

MARCY: I'm afraid I wouldn't have the money to get a list of things.

GRANDMOTHER: They didn't cost any money but gave me more pleasure than if they had cost a great deal of money.

MARCY: Whatever did she give you?

GRANDMOTHER: The list went something like this: I

promise to fix dinner for a whole week and clean up afterwards; I promise to make my bed and straighten my room for one whole month without being reminded; I promise to try to get along with my two brothers for one week; I promise to deliver to my very special mother two hugs and two kisses each morning for one week.

MARCY: That was a very different Mother's Day gift. Did Mother really do all of that?

GRANDMOTHER: She certainly did, and she was a more grown-up daughter forever after.

MARCY: I'm going to do that, too! Thank you so much, Grandma. Maybe the reason Mother is so great is because she had a wonderful mother! *(Kisses GRANDMOTHER. Both exit.)*

No Cornbread Dressing

Puppets: Any two puppets may be used.

SHEP: *(Entering)* **Hi, folks! Did you have a wonderful Thanksgiving like I did?** *(HAPPY JACK appears.)* **Say, there's my friend, Happy Jack. Hi there, ole buddy! Did you have lots to eat Thanksgiving Day?**

HAPPY JACK: *(Disgruntledly)* **Yeah, I had plenty to eat but no pumpkin pie. And what's Thanksgiving without pumpkin pie?**

SHEP: **You poor fellow — no pie for Thanksgiving!**

HAPPY JACK: **Oh, I didn't say I didn't have any pie at all.**

SHEP: **What kind did you have?**

HAPPY JACK: **I had cherry and apple and chocolate and butterscotch and pecan and peach and lemon — but no pumpkin, and that's my favorite.**

SHEP: **But you had lots of turkey and dressing, didn't you?**

HAPPY JACK: *(Dejectedly)* **Yeah — yeah, but not cornbread dressing, and as far as I'm concerned, cornbread dressing is the *only* kind of dressing.**

SHEP: **You weren't very thankful for your Thanksgiving dinner, then?**

HAPPY JACK: **Would you have been? No pumpkin pie and no cornbread dressing!**

SHEP: **Didn't you get enough to eat?**

HAPPY JACK: **Sure, such as it was!**

SHEP: **What did you have, besides all those pies and turkey and non-cornbread dressing, I mean?**

HAPPY JACK: **Candied yams, ham, green beans, corn on the cob, cranberry sauce, stuffed celery sticks, mashed potatoes and giblet gravy, fresh garden salad, hot rolls and butter . . . .**

SHEP: *(Interrupting)* **You have the nerve to complain after a feast like that? You did eat, didn't you?**

HAPPY JACK: **Oh, sure. I forced myself. A fellow has to eat, even if he doesn't have what he wants.**

SHEP: **Happy Jack, I think you forgot what they call last Thursday.**

HAPPY JACK: **I did not! It was Thanksgiving Day. But how could I be thankful when I didn't have pumpkin pie and . . . .**

SHEP: *(Interrupts, mockingly)* . . . and **cornbread dressing!
Happy Jack, you're impossible! Look, you had loads of
delicious food, a roof over your head, you aren't sick
or in trouble . . . .**

HAPPY JACK: *(Interrupting)* **Sure, sure — I know, but still
I didn't have pumpkin pie and cornbread dressing. You
can't *really* expect me to be thankful if I didn't get my
favorite foods.**

SHEP: **I'll tell you what, there's lots of cornbread dressing
and pumpkin pie left at my house. Come on over and
eat all you want.**

HAPPY JACK: *(Loudly)* **Boo-hoo-hoo, boo-hoo-hoo.**

SHEP: **Now what's the matter?**

HAPPY JACK: **Boo-hoo-hoo. I ate so much other stuff I
don't have room left for any pumpkin pie or cornbread
dressing. Boo-hoo-hoo. This has been a terrible
Thanksgiving — just awful, awful.**

SHEP: **You're hopeless, Happy Jack! Go on home and be
miserable; you've earned it! Goodbye!** *(HAPPY JACK
exits, sobbing.)*

SHEP: **Happy Jack didn't celebrate Thanksgiving, he just
had a Turkey Day. Poor, old, unthankful Happy Jack.
I'm glad *I* had a *Thanksgiving* Day, aren't you?**

CHAPTER 10

The Special Problems of Puppet People

- Freddy Meets Diablo
- A Frog or a Prince?

Freddy Meets Diablo

Puppets: Two frogs, FREDDY and CROAKY; DIABLO, an
orange snake. Snake puppet can be fashioned by making a
slit in the under part — just back of the head — of a large toy
snake and removing part of the stuffing so a hand can be
inserted.

ANNOUNCER: **Freddy Frog is visiting his cousin Croaky
at Marshy Pond.**

(CROAKY and FREDDY appear together.)

CROAKY: **Well, Freddy, how do you think you're going to
like Arizona?**

FREDDY: **It sure is different from Iowa. I mostly stay in
the water to keep from getting sunburned. A frog with
big green blisters would sure look funny.**

CROAKY: **You'll get used to the sun.**

FREDDY: **I suppose so. Say, who else lives in Marshy Pond?
I'd like to meet some of your neighbors.**

CROAKY: **Myrtle the Turtle is nice, a little snappy but a
good friend. But look out for Diablo!**

FREDDY: **Diablo? That's Spanish for devil, isn't it? Who's
Diablo?**

CROAKY: **A big orange snake!** *(If snake puppet is different
color, substitute that color.)* **And his favorite food is tender
young frogs!**

FREDDY: **Aw — I'm not afraid of any ole snake. I can out-
swim all the frogs, turtles and snakes back home.**

CROAKY: **Diablo doesn't depend on how fast he can swim
to catch frogs. He uses his wits.**

FREDDY: **His wits?**

CROAKY: **Yep! That's the reason we call him Diablo. He's
as sneaky as that snake in the Garden of Eden.**

FREDDY: **The Garden of Eden? Where's that?**

CROAKY: **Didn't you ever hear the story in the Bible about
Adam and Eve in the Garden of Eden?**

FREDDY: **No, I can't say that I did. Who told you about it?**

CROAKY: **There's a preacher who comes down here to the
park and teaches Bible stories to the kids every Saturday.**

FREDDY: **Stories from the Bible. What's that?**

CROAKY: **My, my, don't they have preachers in Iowa? The**

Bible is a book about God creating the earth and everything in it. It also tells about God's son, Jesus.

FREDDY: What about the snake in the Garden of Eden?

CROAKY: Oh, yes. God made the first man out of dirt and called him Adam. Then he made Adam a wife named Eve and put them both in the lovely Garden of Eden that God made for them.

FREDDY: *(Impatiently)* But what about the snake?

CROAKY: I'm coming to that! Adam and Eve were very happy until the evil one, the devil, tricked Eve into disobeying God.

FREDDY: Eve must have been awfully dumb.

CROAKY: No more than some people today. He told her that if she ate the fruit God had forbidden them to eat, she would become wise. She and Adam both ate some. They became wise all right! Wise enough to know they were in bad trouble with God! For disobeying, God put them out of their beautiful garden.

FREDDY: So you call the snake here in Marshy Pond Diablo because he's sneaky like that ole snake in the Garden of Eden?

CROAKY: That's right. We frogs have to be real careful or we'll end up being snake food. Now, I've got to go. Have a good time but watch out for old Diablo.

FREDDY: I'm not afraid. I'm too sharp for that ole snake. *(CROAKY exits and FREDDY begins to move leisurely toward the other end of the stage. DIABLO sticks his head up from opposite end of stage from FREDDY. FREDDY sees him instantly and whirls around.)*

DIABLO: Good morning! You're new around here, aren't you?

FREDDY: *(Backing away)* You-you-you're Diablo?!

DIABLO: Is that what they call me around here? Well, I'm not the devil or even like the devil. I'm just a harmless king snake.

FREDDY: Croaky says you eat frogs. I'd better go.

DIABLO: Wait! That's not true! I eat bugs, just like you do.

FREDDY: I gotta go —

DIABLO: *(Beginning to sob)* Just because I'm a s-snake, everyone calls me Diablo and won't have anything to do

with me. Boo-hoo-hoo. I'm so lonesome I could d-die.
Boo-hoo-hoo.

FREDDY: But — but how do I know you just want to be
friends?

DIABLO: *(Inches a little toward FREDDY.)* How would you
like to be called Diablo and have everyone afraid of
you? Boo-hoo-hoo.

FREDDY: Please don't cry.

DIABLO: *(Moves a little closer.)* Boo-hoo-hoo. I knew you
would understand. If I could have just one friend it
would help.

FREDDY: *(Still a little doubtful)* Well — I don't like to see
anyone so sad.

DIABLO: *(Moves a little closer.)* I said to myself when I saw
you, "He won't be mean to me like all the others." At
last I'll have a real friend. I've been so lonely. Boo-hoo-
hoo.

FREDDY: You poor thing! Of course I'll be your friend. I —

CROAKY: *(Yells from Offstage.)* Run, Freddy, run! *(DIABLO
lunges at FREDDY and FREDDY barely escapes, out of sight
of the audience.)*

DIABLO: *(Turns back toward audience.)* Oh, well, you can't
win 'em all. I *almost* caught myself a tender fat frog.
I'm pretty sharp, if I do say so myself. Diablo suits me
about right! Heh-heh-heh! I'm almost as smart as that
snake in the Bible! *(DIABLO exits, chuckling wickedly.)*
(CROAKY and FREDDY appear.)

FREDDY: *(Visibly shaking)* Wow! Diablo nearly got me! I'm
still so scared I'm shaking like a leaf.

CROAKY: I told you, Freddy! Diablo is like that snake in
the Garden of Eden. He had you believing his lies.

FREDDY: Yeah! I won't ever call Eve dumb anymore.
Diablo had me convinced he really wanted a friend
when what he really wanted was *me* — for dinner!
Thanks a lot, Croaky! You saved my life. *(They exit,
shoulder to shoulder, or with arms about each other.)*

A Frog or a Prince?

Puppets: CROAKY: a frog; SHEP, a dog (If a dog puppet is not available, a puppet of any kind could be used, but be sure to change the last lines — where indicated.); MARCY, a girl puppet.
(CROAKY and SHEP appear.)

CROAKY: Hello there, old friend. What brings you down to Marshy Pond?

SHEP: Good morning, Croaky. I'm just out for a stroll around the pond. It's always so pretty here: flowers and trees and water.

CROAKY: Yes, I suppose it is pretty. But I get so tired of all this! The *same* old pond, the *same* old trees, the *same* old *me!*

SHEP: Say, old buddy, you sound downhearted. What gives?

CROAKY: Well — I'm just tired of *everything*, but especially with being a frog!

SHEP: What's wrong with being a frog?

CROAKY: Lots of things! A frog never gets to go places, or see things, or do anything exciting. And besides, look at me! I've got these big, bulging eyes, and I hop around on stupid-looking crooked legs. And look what color I am. Green! Yuk!

SHEP: If you don't like being a frog, what *would* you like to be?

CROAKY: A human! They're tall and walk straight on two legs, and can go anywhere. They aren't confined to a muddy old pond. Yep, if I could be anything I wanted to be, I would be a human, a man!

SHEP: *(Thinking hard)* Well — I heard a story once about a frog that got turned into a prince when a lovely lady kissed him. Who's to say, maybe it would work for you. If you could talk a pretty girl into kissing you, you could at least see if it would work. It's worth a try.

CROAKY: But I could *never* get a pretty girl to kiss *me*. What pretty girl would want to kiss an ugly, old green frog? Boo-hoo-hoo. And it probably wouldn't work anyway! Boo-hoo-hoo!

SHEP: Aw, come on, Croaky, don't take on like that.
Being a frog can't be *that* bad!

CROAKY: *(Wails)* Yes, it is! You don't know! You've never
been an ugly old frog!

SHEP: No — no, I never have. But, wait! *(Excitedly)* Maybe
you won't have to stay a frog! Look! Here comes a very
pretty girl! Stop that blubbering and talk real sweet to
her and see if she'll kiss you.

CROAKY: *(Excited)* Say, she is pretty! If she kissed me, I
should turn into a prince on the spot! Watch me use
my charm!

MARCY: *(Appears)* Good morning. Isn't it lovely down here
by the pond? So cool and refreshing.

SHEP: It sure is. My name's Shep, *(Change names if a different
puppet is used)* and this is my friend, Croaky.

MARCY: I'm glad to meet you both. My name is Marcy. Do
you both live here at the pond?

SHEP: Croaky does, but he doesn't like it here.

MARCY: *(Turning to CROAKY)* You don't? I think it is a
perfectly beautiful place to live.

CROAKY: I guess it is if you're a frog. But I don't want to
be a frog! I want to be a human — a prince. Now, you
are a lovely, beautiful, gorgeous, kindly girl, and if you
would do me one small favor, I would turn into a prince.

MARCY: I think you are trying to flatter me. I'm really not
a lovely, beautiful, gorgeous, kindly girl, you know.

CROAKY: Oh, but you are! So, you lovely, beautiful,
gorgeous, kindly girl, would you please, please do me
one tiny favor?

MARCY: If you stop all that beautiful, gorgeous stuff, I
might.

CROAKY: You'll never be sorry. I promise to shower you
with jewels and gifts when I turn into a prince.

MARCY: *(Doubtfully)* What do I have to do?

CROAKY: Just kiss me once.

MARCY: Oh, I couldn't!

CROAKY: Boo-hoo-hoo. I knew it! You can't bear to kiss
an ugly, old green frog! Boo-hoo-hoo!

MARCY: It isn't that at all! Please don't cry. It's just that
I don't believe a kiss will turn you into a prince.

CROAKY: At least try it and see. Please — please!

MARCY: Oh — all right. *(Kisses him lightly on cheek.)*

CROAKY: *(Backs off and looks at himself and then wails.)* I'm still a frog! It didn't work! Boo-hoo-hoo.

SHEP: That wasn't much of a kiss, just a little peck. Perhaps a real big smack would do the job.

MARCY: I still don't think it will work. That story you heard was just a fairy tale!

CROAKY: Please try, anyway. I want to be a prince so badly. I hate being a frog!

MARCY: *(Reluctantly)* **Very well. Here goes.** *(Gives him a loud smack on cheek.)*

CROAKY: *(Backs off and looks at himself again and then wails.)* Boo-hoo-hoo. It didn't work! I'm still a frog!

MARCY: Of course you are! And what's so bad about that?

CROAKY: Boo-hoo-hoo. I hate being an ugly, green frog with big eyes! I even hate eating bugs! I want to be a human! Boo-hoo-hoo.

MARCY: You know — you are being an old silly! You are something special that God made. Did you know that?

CROAKY: No-o-o. How can an old frog be special?

MARCY: God made you special. You are a lovely green color that fits in with the plants and water. God gave you a taste for bugs so you could help him keep things in balance. If it wasn't for you and other bug eaters, insects would eat up every plant and tree in the whole world!

CROAKY: Well-l-l, that makes sense. Did you really mean it when you said I was a lovely color?

MARCY: Sure I did! And look at those special, strong legs God gave you to swim with. No human can swim and jump like you! And even your big eyes are for a purpose. You should be glad you are a frog, because you are just exactly what God wanted and needed when he made you.

CROAKY: You mean a human couldn't take my place?

MARCY: Of course not! You are special because God made you that way. It would be a dull world if we all looked just alike.

SHEP: You can say that again!

CROAKY: Wow! I am something special! Wow! I feel great!
I'm glad I'm a frog! Say, you two have really helped me.
How about having lunch with me? I'll spread you out
the best meal of grasshoppers and water bugs you ever
saw. Yum, yum!

MARCY: Well — no. Thanks a lot, but I really must get
home. Mother was baking a cherry pie when I left.

SHEP: Me neither, Croaky. Thanks anyway. I don't mean
to hurt your feelings, but a big juicy bone is more to
my liking. *(If puppet is not a dog, make the appropriate food
choice adjustment.)*

CROAKY: Everyone to his own poison, they say. Bugs for
me, bones for Shep, and pies for Marcy. But personally,
I think mine sounds the best. Bones and pies? Yuk!
I'm sure glad I'm a frog!

About the Author
BEA CARLTON

Bea Carlton's passion for writing began early in life. High school journalism and English classes received the most attention (and the best grades) from this aspiring writer. Following her instincts, she pursued writing into adulthood. Now a well-established and long-time successful writer, her novels weave a rich blend of mystery, adventure, romance and faith. The fruitful results of her efforts have been eight published novels and avidly loyal readers. Her books have proved to be immensely popular. Two more novels have been accepted for publication.

Her first two novels were best sellers for the publisher. The first book, *In the House of the Enemy,* has been recorded on audio tapes for the visually handicapped by the Society for the Blind.

She lectures regularly for various clubs and writers' groups. She periodically writes articles for regional newsletters and magazines.

Serving as a pastor's wife (though husband Mark is now retired), Bea Carlton found puppetry to be a very effective aid in support of her husband's work. After taking a workshop on puppet making several years ago, she is still hooked! Using puppets in Bible studies and church meetings, she ended up writing most of her own plays. She draws on her valuable ministry contact with people for inspiration in writing her play scripts. This is her third published book on puppets. At one time she felt that puppetry would be too difficult to do. She now shares her enthusiasm and experience in this book so that *You Can Do Christian Puppets* and love it, too!

ORDER FORM

MERIWETHER PUBLISHING LTD.
P.O. BOX 7710
COLORADO SPRINGS, CO 80933
TELEPHONE: (719) 594-4422

Please send me the following books:

_____**You Can Do Christian Puppets #CC-B196**   **$10.95**
by Bea Carlton
A basic guide to Christian puppetry

_____**Learning With Puppets #CC-B136**   **$8.95**
by Hans and Karl Schmidt
An illustrated guide to making puppets in the classroom

_____**Teaching With Bible Games #CC-B108**   **$10.95**
by Ed Dunlop
20 "kid-tested" contests for Christian education

_____**No Experience Necessary! #CC-B107**   **$12.95**
by Elaine Clanton Harpine
A "learn by doing" guide for creating children's worship

_____**Where Does God Live? #CC-B189**   **$8.95**
by Ted Lazicki
Fifty-eight children's sermons for worship

_____**The Official Sunday School Teachers**
Handbook #CC-B152   **$9.95**
by Joanne Owens
An indispensable aid for anyone involved in Sunday school activities

_____**Divine Comedies #CC-B190**   **$12.95**
by T. M. Williams
A collection of plays for church drama groups

_____**Sermons Alive! #CC-B132**   **$12.95**
by Paul Neale Lessard
52 dramatic sketches for worship services

**These and other fine Meriwether Publishing books are available at
your local Christian bookstore or direct from the publisher. Use the
handy order form on this page.**

NAME: _____

ORGANIZATION NAME: _____

ADDRESS: _____

CITY: _____ STATE: _____ ZIP: _____

PHONE: _____

☐ **Check Enclosed**
☐ **Visa or MasterCard #**_____
                                    Expiration
*Signature:*_____ *Date:*_____
           (required for Visa/MasterCard orders)

COLORADO RESIDENTS: Please add 3% sales tax.
SHIPPING: Include $2.75 for the first book and 50¢ for each additional book ordered.

☐ *Please send me a copy of your complete catalog of books and plays.*